Situation-Reaction Drills
for Offensive Basketball

Situation-Reaction Drills for Offensive Basketball

RICHARD W. HARVEY

Parker Publishing Company, Inc.
West Nyack, New York

Library of Congress Cataloging in Publication Data

Harvey, Richard W.
  Situation-reaction drills for offensive basketball.

  Includes index.
  1. Basketball—Offense. 2. Basketball—Training.
3. Basketball—Coaching. I. Title.
GV889.H37 1983   796.32'32   83-4084
ISBN 0-13-811273-8

DEDICATION

To my Father

Without his guidance and encouragement
my career in athletics, teaching, and
coaching would not have been possible.

Acknowledgments

I want to express my gratitude to all the fine young men I have had the opportunity to coach. The players have given me insight into coaching techniques and have created an atmosphere to make improved modifications and variations in practice procedure.

I have been fortunate to have excellent assistant coaches over the years. I greatly appreciate their loyalty and hard work to make the total basketball program a success.

I want to especially acknowledge the assistance of my teaching colleague, Sara M. Staub, for her valuable time spent in proofreading the manuscript and preparing it in the current vernacular.

How this book will help you

Basketball has always been and will always be a game of fundamental skill development and execution. The most elaborate and intricate offensive systems are rendered ineffective unless each individual player can recognize and react appropriately to situations created by the opposition.

Most coaches can let the "graphite fly," have the "chalk talk," and design extremely imaginative offenses. On paper there is an answer for every defensive system employed.

At the high school level of competition where coaches often cannot control the talent flow, it is essential that fundamental skill development receive major concentration. Year in and year out some coaches consistently produce a competitive squad whether the cycle flow of talent is up or down. Analyzing their success will show the constant repetition of drills and concentration on fundamental basketball skills in their practice sessions. When a game winds down to the closing minutes and final seconds, the outcome is determined by the team that reacts faster and executes more effectively the fundamental skills.

The efficient execution of offensive basketball skills is developed through repetitive practice in forming habit actions and reactions to the situations that will occur during the course of a game. The primary way to accomplish these objectives and goals is to expose the players daily to as many of these conditions as possible in structured drill situations. Three ingredients are absolutely necessary to do this. First, you must spend a great deal of time organizing and planning small group participation, which includes various skills and appropriate action-reaction situations. Second, a strict time allotment must be utilized to allow for complete coverage of all material in teaching exactness and efficiency in performance. Third, you must be able to stimulate the players to work at peak effort continuously through competitive and pressure conditions developed for that specific purpose. There is much more to practice than just scrimmaging, shooting, and free-lance organization if you want to develop a successful basketball program.

R.W.H.

THE PURPOSE OF THIS BOOK

To build a structurally sound basketball program, skills must be firmly established in a systematic step-by-step progression through fundamentals and drill concentration. After emphasizing and developing skill patterns, elaborate and intricate systems of play can then come into focus. However, types of systems are irrelevant until the individual- and team-related skills can be executed properly. Habit formation through practice exposure can develop more effective and quicker reactions to the situations that may occur.

For every action in the game of basketball, there is a necessary reaction. Conversely, there are selective actions that are initiated by the positions of players, possession of the basketball, and status of the game in relation to time and score.

This book will provide insight, knowledge, and practice ideas to develop offensive basketball skills through a concentrated drill program.

Contents

Situation-Reaction Drills
for Offensive Basketball

1
Developing the conditioning aspects of basketball

The nature of the sport of basketball is running. Without proper conditioning, players may experience injury, excessive body fatigue, or abnormal strain placed on various systems in the body causing illness and other related problems.

Practices must be structured to develop overall body conditioning so that the actual games will be less strenuous and physically demanding than the daily practice session. This will help the body to withstand the physical stresses of competition.

If a player wore a pedometer during a normal practice session, I would expect a minimum distance of five miles traveled. Naturally, the distance would vary in speed, direction, and effort expended during the different organized phases of practice. Therefore, it is essential to provide the proper environment to train the players properly so that their bodies will respond to the conditions created by the starting, stopping, and running aspects of basketball. Conditioning for endurance, strength, power, and explosiveness provides the foundation for developing efficiency in body movement and the ability to withstand fatigue.

The drills in this chapter are devoted to the conditioning phase necessary for successful performance. But conditioning is also the toughest of tasks, and therefore variations in drills and techniques are essential in relieving boredom, staleness, and player discontent.

FLEXIBILITY

Flexibility is a measure of the range of movement in a joint and varies with each individual. In most cases the flexibility of an individual can be improved beyond the present capabilities.

Work on Down

Players spread and stand with their legs together, feet flat on the floor, and knees locked. The hands are placed on the knees and held for a count of five. This movement starts to loosen the lower back and hamstring area. After five seconds, the hands are moved down the shin area and also held for a count of five. The hands are eventually worked down to the ankles, and an attempt is made to pull the head into the knees and hold for a count of five.

Four-Way Stretch

Players spread their legs apart to the side as wide as possible with both feet remaining flat on the floor. The hands are placed on the floor in front of the body for support. The body is rocked forward shifting the weight toward the toes with the heels remaining in contact with the floor. The rocking is reversed until the weight is back on the heels. The toes still remain in contact with the floor. The forward-backward rocking motion continues in a slow, rhythmic movement pattern. This exercise stretches the inside of the thigh and the hip area. The second phase of stretching from this position is to lean left and then right, always remembering to keep the feet flat on the floor and hands in position for support.

Wide Stride

Players stand with their legs spread far apart in a wide stance. The feet are flat on the floor with the knees locked. The body is bent forward at the waist. The arms are folded behind the back. Players hold this stretch moving the head toward the floor. This movement aids in stretching the lower back, back of the legs, and the hip region.

Variations: The arms are folded in front of the body and an attempt is made to touch the elbows to the floor.

Another stretching maneuver from this position is to extend the arms straight back with the elbows locked. Both arms are then raised together by lifting upward from the shoulders. This movement helps to loosen the arms, shoulders, and upper back area.

Rock and Roll

Players stand with feet flat on the floor and legs spread wide. The knees are bent at a 90-degree angle and the hands are placed on the head. Players start rocking forward as far as possible without losing balance or moving the feet. The same movement is continued in a clockwise fashion by moving to the right as far as possible. The next movement is to the rear and then left to complete the circle. After three clockwise rotations, the movement proceeds in a counterclockwise direction.

Achilles Stretching

Players sit on the floor in an "L" position. The legs are straight in front of the body with the toes pointing toward the ceiling. Hands are placed on the floor at the side of the body for balance and support. On command, the toes are pulled back and held for a five-second count. After a brief rest, the toes are pointed away from the body and held for a five-second count. The alternating pushing and pulling of the toes is repeated three times. The second phase is to roll the legs out so that the outsides of the feet are flat on the floor. From this position the pulling and pushing of the toes is continued for five counts and repeated three times. The final phase of this exercise is done with the legs turned in so that the insides of the feet are flat on the floor. Once again the toes are pushed and pulled toward the body for five-second periods in the same fashion that the first two phases were executed.

Groin Stretching

Players sit on the floor with their knees bent and legs spread apart. The toes are clasped by the hands and the feet are brought as close as possible to the buttocks. Once in this position, two movements are executed to stretch the inside of the thigh. First, players attempt to press knees to the floor. Second, players push knees to floor and bend over from waist trying to touch forehead to feet. Extremely flexible players may be able to force the outside of the legs to touch the floor for total stretching.

Calf Stretching

Players stand in a forward staggered position with the legs. The knee of the lead leg is flexed. A step forward with the lead leg is taken as far as possible while maintaining a straight trail leg with the rear foot remaining flat on the floor. This position is continued until tension is felt in the calf area of the rear leg. The position is held for five counts and then the lead and trail legs are exchanged to provide sufficient stretching for both.

Ankle Extension

Players stand with their legs together and knees locked. On command, players jump by pushing with the feet and ankles only as legs remain locked in position. The weight is rocked forward on to the toes before the ankle extension is executed. Five jumps are done in succession followed by a brief rest period. Three sets of jumps are performed. The amount of forceful extension and the number of repetitions are increased daily to strengthen the ankles. An important point to remember is to land on the toes first followed by a roll back on the heels before preparing for the next jump. Landing flat-footed is contraindicated as this may stress the lower back and cause a possible injury or extreme soreness.

Sitting Stance

Players stand with their feet flat on the floor and legs shoulder width apart. They start by bending their knees and dropping the buttocks as if starting to sit down. When the thighs reach a parallel position to the floor, movement stops and the back is straightened. This position is held for thirty seconds. The length of time is increased by five seconds in each succeeding practice session.

Variation: While assuming the stance, the players hold a basketball above the head.

ENDURANCE

Endurance is the ability to exert muscular force repeatedly over a period of time.

Wall Touch

Players pair off and line up outside the end line at one end of the court. On your signal, the first group of players sprint to touch the wall at the far end of the gym and return quickly to the end of the line. Always establish a time limit to provide incentive for maximum expenditure of effort. Pairs alternate sprinting on your command. Increase the number of repetitions daily to develop the endurance level for sustained effort within the designated time limit established.

Variations: Players touch four walls (down and back twice). The time required is double the two wall time plus two seconds. Six walls are touched in triple time plus four seconds. An endurance series of two walls-four walls-six walls-eight walls-ten walls-eight walls-six walls-four walls-two walls is an excellent conditioner. Players do wall touches while dribbling a ball with extra time allotted for completion.

Forward and Return

Players pair off and line up outside the end line. The groups of partners alternate running. On command, the first group sprints forward to touch the free throw line and immediately back pedals to the end line. Upon touching, direction is reversed again sprinting forward to touch half court followed by a back pedal returning to the end line. After touching, players sprint forward to the far free throw line and then back pedal back to the end line. Finally, players sprint full court forward to the far end line and back pedal back to the starting position. A time limit is established to motivate players to expend a solid effort.

Variation: Players execute the same running maneuvers while dribbling a basketball.

Forward and Reverse

Players pair off and form two running groups on the end line. On command, the first group sprints to touch the free throw line. Immediately after touching, they reverse direction by back pedaling to the end line. Upon touching, they spring forward to the midcourt line and then back pedal to the free throw line. Next they sprint to the far free throw line and back pedal to the midcourt line. Finally, they sprint to the end line and back pedal to the original starting position. Establish a time limit for completion of the run based on the ability and basic speed of the squad.

Variations: Each line is touched with one hand before reversing direction.

Each line is touched with both hands before reversing direction.

A basketball is dribbled while sprinting the course.

Two basketballs are used in completing the course.

Leg Scissors

Players stand in a forward-backward straddle position with the left leg leading. On command, the legs are switched forward and back as quickly as possible for thirty seconds.

Variations: The feet are shifted so that the heel of the lead foot and the toe of the trail foot make contact with the floor when switching.

The knees are flexed and the shift takes place with the feet landing flat-footed when switching.

The legs are kept straight and the shift occurs with the weight staying on the toes when switching.

Ball Scissors

Players spread out and assume a forward-backward straddle position with the left leg leading. On command, the ball is passed from the right hand to the left hand in a position behind the left leg. Immediately after the ball transfer, the legs are switched bringing the right leg to the forward position. The ball is passed from the left hand back to the right hand behind the right leg. A continuous leg shift and ball exchange is performed as quickly as possible. Designate a time period to place emphasis on concentration, effort, and control.

Running Scissors

Players pair off on the end line with a basketball. Partners alternate turns with one partner from each in group one. The first group starts on the end line holding a basketball, with one leg in advance of the other. On a signal, they proceed to run forward the length of the court. Each time the legs switch positions, the ball is moved behind the lead leg, changing hands. The continuous ball movement running downcourt resembles a figure-eight design. This drill is an extension of the previously explained ball scissors drill with running added. For best results and faster movement, the ball should be moved from the inside lead leg to the outside and then the lead leg is dropped to the rear.

Variation: The running scissors drill is performed while moving backward. The ball is moved from inside the lead leg to the outside and then the lead leg is dropped to the rear.

Sliding Figure Eight

Players pair off on the end line with a basketball and alternate turns. The first group stands facing the side wall so their left shoulders are facing downcourt. On command, the players start sliding laterally to the left. On each successive slide, the ball is circled around both legs in a figure-eight rotation. On returning the players slide to the right while performing the figure-eight maneuver.

Lead Leg Circle

Players pair off on the end line with a basketball and alternate turns. Group one starts with the right leg forward in advance of the left. The ball is circled quickly around the right leg. As soon as the circle is completed, the left leg slides forward to close. Immediately the right leg is extended forward and the ball is circled again. The circle-close-slide forward action continues up and down the floor with the ball always traveling in a circle around the lead leg. The lead leg never changes and the feet do not cross or pass each other at any time.

Variations:
- The left leg is the lead leg.
- The sequence of the sliding action is switched.
- The lead leg slides forward and the ball is circled around the rear leg.
- Another sequence is circling with the lead leg, circling both legs when closing, and circling the lead leg when opening.

STAMINA

Stamina is the ability of the body to withstand and delay fatigue from setting in. Fatigue is the element causing a fall-off in the repeated performance of any activity. The more often a muscle performs a movement in training during practice sessions, against the same resistance and at the same speed required in competition, then the less likely it is to become locally fatigued by that movement during competition.

Running and Tapping

The squad is divided into two lines, single file, at a basket at opposite ends of the court. The first player in each line has a basketball (Diagram 1-1). On your signal, the first player in each line tosses the ball high off the backboard. As soon as the ball is released, the player turns to the right and runs to the end of the opposite line. The second player jumps and taps the ball off the backboard before turning and running to the other line. Each player in turn jumps and taps the ball off the backboard before moving to the other line. The object is to keep both balls in play off the backboard without allowing either ball to drop to the floor. The drill is run for one and one-half minutes and increased each time in succeeding practice sessions. When either ball touches the floor, the watch is stopped and fifteen seconds are added to the time remaining to tap.

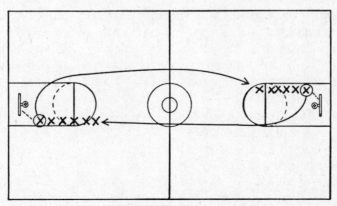

Diagram 1-1

Variations: The players tap with the right hand only.

The players catch and control the ball with two hands before releasing.

Up and Over

Players spread out and place a ball to the side of their right foot on the floor. On a signal, the players start jumping from side to side with both feet over the ball. They move back and forth as quickly as possible for ten seconds. Three sets of the drill are run with a ten-second rest period between each set. The time of consecutive jumping is increased as stamina improves.

Variations: A specific number of consecutive jumps is completed before stopping.

Consecutive jumping is completed until fatigue is evident because of lack of control or loss of balance.

The ball is placed in front of the feet.

Jumping is completed in a forward-backward movement over the ball.

Court Line Touch

Players spread out along the end line holding a basketball. There are five distinctive lines on a basketball court. They include the end line, free throw line, midcourt line, opposite free throw line, and opposite end line.

On your signal, all players sprint to the free throw line, place their ball on the floor, and back pedal to the end line without the ball. All movement is done as quickly as possible. As soon as the end line is touched, players sprint forward to pick up their ball and continue to the midcourt line where the ball is placed on the floor again. Immediately, the players back pedal to the free throw line. Upon touching, direction is changed again as they sprint forward to pick up their ball and advance it to the opposite free throw line where the ball is once again placed on the floor. They quickly back pedal to touch the midcourt line. After touching, they sprint forward picking up the ball and advancing to the opposite end line and placing the ball down again. Back pedaling is completed to the free throw line. Sprinting forward, the players pick the ball up again. Players turn and sprint forward to the free throw line to start the entire sequence over again until they return to the original starting position. After a rest interval equivalent to the time required to complete the circuit is allowed, players start a second series. Three sets of the drill are sufficient to tax the players physically in developing stamina. As the season progresses, more sets may be run depending upon the condition of the players.

POWER

Power can be described as a maximum expenditure of force in a repeated movement, or the ability to expend a maximum amount of energy in a single explosive act.

Spot Touching

Players spread out around the gym standing next to a wall or backboard and facing it. They select a spot and proceed to jump and touch the spot consecutively. As soon as they land, a takeoff from both feet is initiated immediately in an effort to touch the same spot again. The spot is touched ten consecutive times before resting for ten seconds. Three sets of the exercise are run.

Variations: Spot touching is done with the left hand only.
Spot touching is done with the right hand only.
Spot touching is done with both hands simultaneously.
Spot touching is done by alternating left and right hands on each successive jump.

Fatigue Spot Touching

Players spread out around the gym facing a backboard or wall. Each player jumps and picks out a spot by touching. On your signal, the players start jumping and touching their individual spot. They continue jumping and touching until the leg muscles fatigue and no longer respond to supply the necessary force to reach the same spot. As the legs strengthen and conditioning improves, the number of consecutive touches will increase, indicating a measure of improvement in leg power.

Variations: Have the players hold a basketball and spot touch with it.

Ball Bounce Pin

The players pair off at a basket with a ball. Partners take turns alternating three attempts each. The ball is bounced off the floor to the side of the rim and in line with the backboard. As the ball rebounds off the floor, players time their jump to explode up and pin the ball on the backboard. This is done by pinning the ball with the right hand, left hand, and then both hands. Guards or smaller players can perform the drill using a wall if unable to accomplish the pinning technique off the backboard. It might be advisable to start all players on a wall until the necessary timing is developed. A progression would be:

1. Bouncing the ball only to get the "feel" of the ball going in the right direction and reaching the appropriate height.
2. Bouncing the ball and pinning it off the wall while standing on the floor; pinning the ball at face level, overhead, and finally with a full arm extension to develop the proper technique.
3. Performing the bounce, jump, and pin technique in total.

EXPLOSIVENESS

Explosiveness is the ability to stimulate and coordinate various muscle groups to respond in a synchronized fashion in creating a powerful thrust.

Six-Basket Touch

The players line up on the sideline. They start jogging around the court one by one in a counterclockwise direction. As they approach each basket, they gather for an explosive jump to touch the rim or as high as possible on the net or board. The objective is twofold:

1. To coordinate the necessary body movements to gather and release for an explosive jump.
2. To develop a change of pace in preparation for a powerful jump.

After three circuits are run in a counterclockwise direction, the direction is reversed to clockwise.

Touch and Go

The players pair off at a basket with a ball. The basketball is placed on the free throw line. One partner at each basket is standing on the end line underneath the basket with the back to the free throw line. On a whistle from you, players jump to touch the rim or as high as possible to touch the backboard. As soon as they land, they spring to the free throw line. The ball is quickly picked up and immediately advanced back to the basket on one dribble for a layup. Each player rebounds the shot executed, and puts the ball on the free throw line for the partner to take a turn. Players alternate turns and respond quickly to the whistle start.

Variations: Players jump and touch with the right hand. They recover the ball and dribble to the basket with the right hand for a right-handed layup off the backboard.

Players jump and touch with the left hand. They recover the ball and dribble to the basket with the left hand for a left-handed layup.

The ball is placed outside the lane (left or right) even with the basket. Players jump and touch the rim on the whistle. On landing, they quickly locate the ball and pivot to the basket for a layup without dribbling. Pivoting toward the baseline and middle are executed from both sides of the basket. Partners alternate turns.

Continuous Jumping Layups

Players pair off at a basket with a ball. One partner stands in the lane with the basketball in a position to shoot layups. On the whistle, players jump off two feet and make a layup. Landing in a balanced position on the floor, the players then catch the ball. As soon as the ball touches the hands, players jump immediately and shoot another layup. This pattern continues for a series of five layups. Emphasize accuracy by having players concentrate on shooting the layup so that the ball hits the backboard and drops cleanly through the basket without hitting the rim. Partners alternate turns and sides of the basket utilizing the following sequence of layups:

1. Shoot right-handed layups off the backboard from the right side.
2. Shoot left-handed layups off the backboard from the left side.
3. Shoot left-handed layups off the backboard from the right side.
4. Shoot right-handed layups off the backboard from the left side.

Variations: The first layup is shot from a standing position. As the ball is coming through the net, players time the jump to catch the ball and quickly recover in the air to shoot another layup before touching the floor again. The two-shot series is continued for five repetitions before partners alternate.

Two-Ball Tapping

Players pair off around the gym facing a wall and alternate turns using two basketballs. One partner starts by tapping both basketballs off the wall above the head while standing on the floor. The goal is a consecutive number of taps for a period of time designated by you. After proficiency has been achieved while standing, players start jumping and tapping both basketballs off the wall. After sufficient skill is achieved, the third phase is to try and tap both basketballs off the backboard while jumping. This forces players to keep both basketballs over the head while tapping and to develop a full arm extension to keep the balls in play. This is an excellent drill for timing and coordination development.

2
Improving the efficiency of body movements

Basketball is a game of action and reaction. Each situation that occurs in a game is either an action initiated by a specific goal or objective, or a reaction to a previous action of an opponent. In both cases the movement pattern is characterized by some form of starting, stopping, sprinting, jumping, back pedaling, sliding, or changing direction to respond to the specific requirements that will develop. Players cannot specialize in only certain aspects of basketball. The game involves constant movement and each player has to be capable of responding both offensively and defensively as situations dictate. To be competitive in basketball, players must be in top physical condition and possess excellent endurance. Players must be able to conserve energy whenever possible in order to compete at a peak effort over a sustained period of time. Conserving energy, however, does not imply loafing or relaxing during a sequence of action. The key to energy conservation without decreasing intensity or effort is to develop efficiency in the movement pattern by eliminating wasted or unnecessary motion detrimental to the task.

BALANCE

Maintaining body balance is learning how to keep the center of gravity under control within its supporting base. The center of gravity is located in the hip region.

Foot Stand

Players spread out in a random formation. On your command, all players perform a series of one- and two-foot balance stands. They are held for a period of time to check the ability to maintain balance. The series of positions include:

1. Raise on toes and hold with the eyes open.
2. Raise on toes, close eyes and hold.
3. Raise on one foot and hold with the eyes open and then with the eyes closed.
4. Raise on one foot with the other foot bent backward at the knee and hold with the eyes open and then closed.
5. Raise on one foot with the other leg extended in front of the body and hold; do with the eyes open and then closed.
6. Raise on one foot with the other leg bent forward at the knee and upper leg held parallel to the floor. This position is held with both the eyes open and then closed.

Variations: Players perform balancing maneuvers while holding a ball in front of the body, over the head, and behind the body.

Three-Quarter Turn and Return

Players spread out in mass formation allowing themselves enough room to perform. On your command, all players respond together and jump-turn 270 degrees with both feet landing together. Immediately upon landing and maintaining balance, they jump and return in the same direction back to their original position. The objective is to land under control and in balance while eliminating unnecessary foot movements.

Variations: Players hold a basketball while performing jump turns.

A second variation is for players to face away from you and react to a verbal command of direction to execute the maneuver.

Full Turn and Return

Players spread out with plenty of room to execute full turns. On command, players execute a full turn with both feet jumping and landing as in the previous drill. The same conditions and variations are executed in attempting to improve balance and body control in jumping and landing.

EQUILIBRIUM

Equilibrium is the ability to perform body movements while keeping the center of gravity under control.

Heel Click

Players stand with feet about twelve inches apart straddling a painted line on the floor. On your signal, the players jump in the air, click their heels over the line, and land in the original foot position on the floor. As players develop quicker foot reaction, they jump lower to the floor until they are just clearing the floor while clicking their heels. The drill is run for a ten-second period.

Variations: Players straddle a bamboo pole supported six inches above the floor. The heel-click action is performed over the pole before returning to the floor.

Crisscross Return

Players stand with feet shoulder width apart and hold a ball out in front of the body. On command, all players jump and cross left foot in front of right foot and land with feet crossed. After landing, players jump again and return feet to the original position. Jumping again, the right foot is crossed in front of the left to land. The final jump has feet moving back to the original position. The four-count jumping sequence is continuous as the feet are switched back and forth as quickly as possible.

Variations: Players hold the ball behind the back while performing the drill.
Players hold the ball overhead while performing the drill.

Slide-Step-Pivot-Recover

Players spread out in random formation with a basketball. On your signal, the players slide one step laterally in the direction designated. After completion of the single slide step, a forward pivot is executed on the lead foot. After pivot is completed, another slide step is executed in that direction with a forward pivot back to the original position facing you. The entire movement sequence is done continuously and as quickly as possible under control. Continue with a new direction when all players have returned.

   Variations: Players execute a reverse pivot after the slide step.
   Players start with their back to you and react to a verbal command for the direction and type of pivot to execute.

Step Reaction

   Players spread out and assume an athletic stance with the feet comfortably apart, knees flexed, and the center of gravity low for balance and control. Use a hand signal to designate the direction of movement (left-right-forward-back). Players respond by moving as quickly as possible in a step-slide-close action in the desired direction and then resume their original stance in readiness for the next command.

   Variations: Players stand with their back to you and respond to a verbal command.
   Players hold a ball in front of the body in an offensive threat position while reacting to the designated movement action.

FOOTWORK EFFICIENCY

   Footwork efficiency is the ability to move the feet as quickly as possible in a coordinated motion and under control when changing body position.

Quick Feet

   Players spread out in random formation facing you. They execute one of three maneuvers designated by you. In each movement, concentration is on moving the feet as fast as possible while keeping the feet as close as possible to the floor.

   1. Run. The feet are lifted in place in a quick pitter-patter type movement for ten seconds.
   2. Split. Players start with feet shoulder width apart. The feet are closed together just short of contact and immediately returned. The feet are closed and opened as fast as possible for ten seconds.

3. Shift. Players stand with their feet six inches apart in a parallel stance. Feet are shifted forward and back so that the heel of the lead foot is in line with the toe of the trail foot. A rapid shifting of feet takes place for ten seconds.

Drop-Step Recover

Players spread out and respond to a verbal command or hand signal. The players execute the following sequence of maneuvers. From a defensive stance position with feet parallel, the designated foot is dropped a half-step to the rear followed immediately by a 90-degree reverse pivot to return feet to the parallel position (Diagram 2-1).

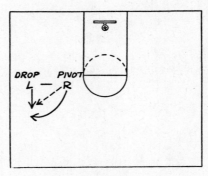

Diagram 2-1

Jump Step-Charge Position

Players spread out in random formation facing you. Hold a basketball in an offensive threat position. Execute fakes and feints to test the defensive balance of the players as they react to these maneuvers in maintaining their stance. As you put the ball on the floor to dribble either left or right, each player responds by slide jumping with both feet landing simultaneously to assume a position with the head on the ball to pick up an offensive charge. Pick the ball up again and repeat faking maneuvers before starting a dribble to initiate the potential charge position. It is important to develop proper mechanics to lessen the blow when contact would occur in "taking the charge." Therefore, when the players execute the slide-jump technique they should also develop the art of drop-stepping to the rear with the preferred foot to lessen the chance of injury on contact. Timing is very important.

EFFECTIVE WEIGHT SHIFTING

Effective weight shifting is the ability to improve the rate at which body position is changed to gain a proper alignment in producing leverage and regaining control of the center of gravity for balance.

Quick Hopping

Players spread out in random formation facing you. On command, the players execute a quick two-foot hop in the designated direction. The sequence of continuous hopping is three hops forward, three hops backward, three hops left, and three hops right as quickly as possible. When finished, players resume a ready position to start again.

Variation: Players hold a ball in front of the body, overhead, or behind the back while hopping in the prescribed sequence.

A second variation is to decrease the number of hops in the four directions as each sequence is completed.

Side to Side Over Line

Players spread out and stand next to a line on the floor. On command, the players jump with both feet together side to side across the line as quickly as possible for seven seconds. Next, the players face the line and jump forward and backward as fast as possible for seven seconds. The third time they execute a quarter-turn over the line and back.

Variation: A basketball is held in different positions (overhead, straight out in front, behind back, straight down in front) while executing the three jumping maneuvers.

Letter Jumping

Players spread out in random formation. On command, players form a designated letter by executing the appropriate jumping maneuver necessary to complete the movement pattern. Also, each succeeding jump within the formation is completed as quickly as possible upon landing.

1. The letter "I" is a long jump forward followed by a vertical jump to dot the "I."

2. The letter "V" is a long jump forward followed by a long jump backward at a 45-degree angle either left or right.
3. The letter "W" is a long jump backward, long jump forward at 45 degrees, a long jump backward at 45 degrees. A "W" is completed to the right and then the left.
4. Additional letters to form are L, M, N, Z.

ACCELERATION

Acceleration is the ability to move from a stopped or resting position to peak speed in a short period of time.

Toss Ball—Recover

Players spread out along the end line with a ball. Each player tosses the ball with slight backspin about ten feet in front of the body. The ball is kept below head level. After the ball bounces, each player accelerates to recover the ball with a two-foot jump stop before the ball bounces a second time. The same technique is continued until the players have traveled the full length of the floor and back. Concentration is on accelerating and stopping in balance.

Variations: Players work in pairs starting on the end line with one basketball. One player is approximately ten feet in front of a partner and facing downcourt. The player behind tosses the ball out to the right or left of the partner. The front player accelerates after the first bounce and recovers the ball with a two-foot jump stop before the ball bounces a second time. The distance of the throw on each succeeding toss is lengthened to force the player to accelerate at peak effort for the recovery.

A second variation is for the partners to face each other at a distance of ten feet. Each player alternates turns tossing the ball to the right, left or short of the partner. The recovering player waits until the first ball bounce before accelerating to the ball.

Blue and White

Players are paired off back to back across the court at the half-court line (Diagram 2-2). Each pair is assigned a number. A ball is placed at the free throw line of both baskets. You call a number. The corresponding pair reacts and accelerates toward the basket they are facing. The ball is scooped up and taken in on one dribble for a

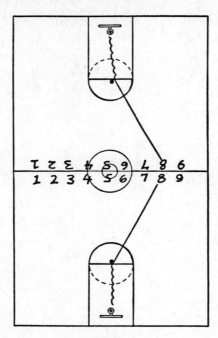

Diagram 2-2

layup. Competition is involved by keeping score by teams. Players must let the ball hit the floor after passing through the net to determine the winner. The losing player or team may be assigned a penalty run.

> **Variation:** Players dribble a ball in place at midcourt. When their number is called, both players accelerate on a sprint dribble and drive for a layup.

Timed Layup

Players stand outside the end line with the exception of one player who stands inbounds inside the foul lane. A manager stands out of bounds under the basket with a number of balls available. You stand on the side line with a stop watch. On command, the manager passes a ball inbounds to the player on the court. The receiver turns and dribbles as fast as possible full court for a layup. The stopwatch is started when the ball is touched inbounds and stopped when the ball is released for a layup. Players go one after another with a right-hand drive first and then a left-hand drive the second time through. The purpose of the drill is to show players how little time it takes to drive the full length of the court for a layup.

Variation: A defensive player guards the inbounds player in a denial position. The receiver must work to get free before getting the pass and driving for a layup.

Lean and Recover

Players line up straddling the midcourt line with a basketball, facing you. You are out of bounds on the side line (Diagram 2-3).

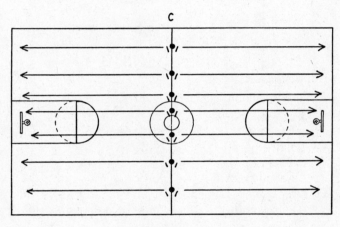

Diagram 2-3

Balls are placed in front of the players on the midcourt line. Every player has both hands placed on their ball in a leaning position with the weight shifted forward. On command, each player immediately picks up the ball and accelerates to the end line in the direction you signal. Players then walk back to midcourt and assume the original leaning position ready to react again. A single elimination contest can be run to determine the quickest player after every player has had several opportunities in both directions.

Variations: Players watch you on the side line and receive a visual signal to react.

Players stand with their backs to you and receive a verbal signal to react.

IMAGE SKILL DEVELOPMENT

An essential ingredient for improvement in skill development involves the utilization of imagery. Players must be able to visualize and "feel" the proper mechanics of skill execution. Practicing an offensive technique without a basketball will reduce physical error while improving mental concentration to implant the proper sequence of movements. In developing the mental picture of the skill, it is important to limit the major check points to body position, balance, hand position, and completion of the act. This will help reduce confusion and misunderstanding on the part of the players.

There are seven skills that are the nucleus to becoming a complete offensive player.

1. Free throw shooting motion
2. Layup shooting technique
3. Jump shooting technique
4. Dribbling techniques and maneuvers
5. Passing motion
   (a) chest pass
   (b) bounce pass
   (c) overhead pass
   (d) baseball pass
6. Driving techniques
   (a) jab step
   (b) crossover step
   (c) rocker step
7. Assuming proper screening position

Players spread out in mass random formation. They execute and repeat the same skill without a basketball on your command. A second method is for you to verbally call the different skills with the players responding in mass.

3
Improving the effectiveness of movement patterns

The specific areas of concentration needed to develop effective action-reaction movement includes agility, changing direction quickly, coordination, quickness, anticipation, kinesthesis, and ambidexterity. The drills in this section are designed to improve these skill areas by giving players an opportunity to experience the different types of movement patterns inherent in the game of basketball. They will also be able to experiment and realize the most efficient movement that will be dictated by individual body build.

COORDINATION

Coordination is the ability to coordinate simultaneous actions of different body parts as efficiently as possible without any unnecessary tension that would interfere with a smooth sequence of muscle action to complete the act.

Switch Feet in Place

Players spread out with plenty of room to execute the drill. Each player stands in a forward-stride position with the left foot in advance of the right. On command, all players switch legs forward and back. Each time the legs change position, the hands are clapped between. The speed of movement is increased with the switching and hand clapping occurring as quickly as possible for a ten-second interval.

Variation: The legs are parallel and moved in a side-stride action, as in a jumping jack, and back together. The hands are held with one in front of the body and one behind. The knees are flexed and the body bent at the waist for balance. Each time the legs are parted to the side, the hands are clapped between the legs. On each succeeding clap, the hands are reversed in front and back for the clap. The drill is performed as quickly as possible for ten seconds.

Hop-Dribble Series

Each player spreads out along the end line facing downcourt with a ball. On your command and direction, the players remain in place and perform the following sequence of maneuvers:

1. Hopping on the left foot and dribbling with the left hand.
2. Hopping on the right foot and dribbling with the right hand.
3. Hopping on the left foot and dribbling with the right hand.
4. Hopping on the right foot and dribbling with the left hand.
5. Hopping on both feet and crossover dribbling from left to right and right to left on each hop.

Variation: The previous sequence of movements are performed while moving forward the length of the court and back.

A second variation is to execute the sequence while hopping backward.

Slow-Fast Exchange

Players spread out with a ball. On command, each player dribbles the ball as fast as possible with the right hand while picking up the feet as slowly as possible in place. Trying to regulate two varying speeds with different body parts is extremely difficult and improves coordination as well as concentration. The same is done while dribbling first with the left hand and finally while alternating left-right dribbling on alternate bounces. The second phase of the drill is to dribble slowly and move the feet as quickly as possible.

Variations: The ball is dribbled low and the feet are raised high.

The ball is dribbled high and the feet are raised by bending at the knees. The heels are brought as closely as possible to the buttocks.

Wall Dribble

All players spread out around the gym facing a wall at a distance of three feet, with a ball. Each player starts dribbling off the wall by extending the arm so the ball is about four inches away. The ball is dribbled around in front of the body from side to side and up and down with both the left and right hands. Once mastery has been established in keeping the ball in play, the eyes are closed to develop a "feel" for dribbling.

Variations: The ball is dribbled above the head off the wall with the eyes open and then closed.

The ball is dribbled off the wall below the waist with the fingers pointed down.

The ball is dribbled off the wall in front of the face while alternating left and right hands as fast as possible with the eyes both open and closed.

Jump Rope Maneuvers

Every player has a jump rope and is spread out with plenty of room to maneuver. The players perform a series of maneuvers on your command as outlined below:

1. Rhythm and tempo jump. The jumping is with a short skip-hop between in preparation for the next jump. This continues for a specified period of time.
2. A speed jump. The jump rope is moved as rapidly as possible but with jumping only once on each full cycle around the body.
3. Rapid rope jumping. A jump is performed for height while the rope is moved as fast as possible to see how many times the rope can be passed under the feet before landing.
4. Isolated jumping. Jumping is on the left foot only followed by jumping on the right foot only.

Variations: Players line up on the end line with a jump rope. The first technique is to run forward and jump rope the length of the court and back.

The next variation is to hop full court on the left foot and back. The same procedure is followed with the right foot.

A third variation is to hop full court on both feet and back.

A final variation is to hopscotch (hop left-hop right-hop both) full court and back.

AGILITY

Agility is the ability to change body position and direction quickly, keeping the center of gravity under control at all times.

Turn-Recover-Shoot

Players pair off at a basket. One partner stands at the free throw line with a ball and faces the basket. The other partner stands under the basket with the back to the free throw line. On your whistle, the player at the free throw line immediately passes the ball toward the partner under the basket. At exactly the same time the whistle sounds, the receiver turns to locate quickly the incoming pass. Upon reception and control, a layup is executed without taking a dribble. Each player receives three to five passes before exchanging positions.

Variations: The passer throws a chest pass, bounce pass, underhand flip pass, or an overhead pass. Variations for the receiver include:

1. Executing a two-foot jump turn to the right and left to receive the pass.
2. Pivoting on the right and left foot to receive the pass.

Up and Back

Players pair off at a basket. One partner stands with a ball at the free throw line. The other partner stands on the end line under the basket and faces out of bounds. The ball is placed on the floor near the free throw line. On a whistle, the end line player turns and sprints to pick up the basketball. One dribble is taken back to the basket for a layup as quickly as possible. The shot is rebounded without letting it touch the floor and passed back to the partner at the free throw line. The ball is placed on the free throw line again as the shooter returns to the end line waiting for another whistle. After several opportunities recovering the ball and driving left or right, players switch positions.

Middle Player Lead

Players are organized in three lines equidistant apart on the end line (Diagram 3-1). The first player in each line works in a group of three with the other two lines. The middle person is the leader of the drill. This player starts moving downcourt and at any time during the fifteen-second time period may change direction, speed, or type of movement (slide-back pedal-shuffle-gallop-skip-high knee action-pivot-jump-hop, etc.). The other two members of the group respond to the movement pattern and execute the same maneuver as quickly as they perceive the specific action. Players rotate lines when finished.

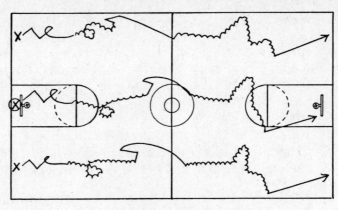

Diagram 3-1

Variations: Players move without a ball, with one ball, and using two balls.

QUICKNESS

Quickness is the ability to respond to a cue and immediately initiate the appropriate muscle movement in preparation for the next required action.

Quarter Turn Recover

Players spread out with a ball and face you. On a visual or sound command the players jump one quarter-turn with both feet left or right. Upon landing, they immediately jump and return back to the original position facing you. The object is to turn and return as quickly as possible in balance and under control.

Variations: Players turn, slam a ball to the floor, and catch before returning to the original position.

The next variation is for the players to start with their back to you and respond to a verbal command on the direction of the turn.

A final variation is for the players to drop the ball, turn in the appropriate direction, return, and regain control of the ball before it bounces again.

Half-Turn Recover

Players spread out with a ball and face you. On various types of commands the players execute a half-turn while performing the same maneuvers outlined in the previous drill.

Listen and Turn

Players pair off with a ball. One partner stands holding the ball in front of the body. The partner stands with the back to the ball. The partner with the ball drops it to the floor. The reacting partner listens for the ball to bounce off the floor. Upon hearing the bounce, the player immediately jump turns to locate the ball and catch it before it bounces a second time. Players are instructed to turn both ways. Also, the ball is dropped from head level at the beginning. As success of recovery is achieved, each succeeding drop should be lowered until the ball is dropped from the knee level.

Variation: Silently point to the player or players who should drop the ball. Respective partners respond to the sound and turn to recover the ball.

REACTION

Reaction is the ability to respond to a stimulus or situation and initiate the appropriate response as quickly as possible.

Mirror Image Drill

Players pair off around the court. One player is designated as the "initiator" and the partner as the "reactor." The initiator performs isolated skills or movement patterns with the arms and legs. The partner "mirrors" the image by responding as quickly as the cue becomes apparent with the identical response. After a period of time or specific number of movements, partners switch roles.

Variation: Both partners have a ball. One player initiates the movement pattern by changing ball position around the body. Partners react to execute the same movements with their basketballs.

Partners Pair Off

Partners pair off with a ball. They stand facing each other in an offensive-defensive stance at a distance approximately arms length apart. One player dribbles a ball in front of the partner. The partner is in a proper defensive stance with arms extended toward the ball. On a whistle, a simultaneous offensive-defensive reaction takes place. The dribbler attempts to protect the ball by pulling it away from the defender by continuing dribbling using a pull-back, crossover, or reverse maneuver. The defender reacts accordingly and attempts to steal or knock the ball away before the dribbler can successfully protect the ball. After several attempts with both hands dribbling, partners switch offensive and defensive roles.

Defensive Stance—Position

Players spread out in random formation and face you. There are three defensive stance alignments determined by the offensive player's potential actions. When the offensive player is dribbling, the defender has both hands low outside the line of the knee with palms facing up. When the offensive player is in a shooting position, the defender raises both hands over the head in a contesting position. When the offensive player is in a threat position (all options available), the defender takes a position with one hand high and one low (the hand opposite the ball or strong hand of the opponent). Use three commands to dictate changes in positioning. All players react as fast as possible to assume the dribble-shot-threat defensive positioning on the ball with the appropriate hand positioning.

Anatomy Touch

Players spread out with a basketball and face you. Four specific areas of the body are numbered for the drill: one is the shoulders; two is the stomach; three is the buttocks; four is the knees. Each player holds a ball with arms straight in front of the body. Call one through four randomly. On each number call the players drop the basketball, touch the designated area of the body with their hands, and recatch the ball before it hits the floor. Immediately the ball is returned to the fully extended position while waiting for the next number call. A single elimination contest can be run with the players.

CHANGE OF DIRECTION

Changing direction involves the ability to change the momentum of the body and initiate it in a new direction as efficiently as possible while keeping the center of gravity under control.

Line Cross and Touch

Players are lined up in single file spread out the length of the floor and bisecting the free throw lane (Diagram 3-2). On your command, all players sprint to their right and touch the floor outside of the lane with their palms. Immediately upon touching, each player changes direction and sprints across the lane with the palms again. The back and forth sprinting and touching continues at peak effort for a ten-second interval. A short rest interval is followed by repetition of the drill.

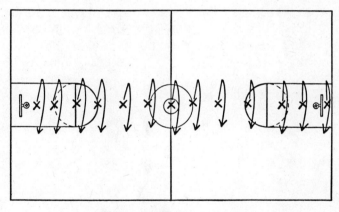

Diagram 3-2

Variations: Players carry a basketball across the lane and either have it touch to floor or slam bounce it before returning.

Another variation is for the players to slide their feet back and forth across the lane.

A final variation is for the players to back pedal across the lane, pivot, and touch before returning.

Ball Over Rim

Players pair off at a basket with one ball. One partner takes the ball and stands outside the foul lane on either side of the basket. The ball is thrown off the backboard over the basket to the other side. The player immediately moves across the lane after releasing the ball and recatches the ball outside the lane with a two-foot jump stop. Immediately upon receiving the ball, a pivot is executed and the ball is quickly thrown back to the other side off the backboard again and recovered. The maneuver is done back and forth five times. On the fifth reception, the player pivots to the basket and makes a bank shot. The other partner then takes a turn performing the drill.

Variations: Players start the drill from the right side of the basket so that on the fifth reception a left-handed bank shot will be taken from the left side.

Players start the drill from the left side of the basket so that on the fifth reception a right-handed bank shot will be taken from the right side of the basket.

Another variation is for the players to alternate pivoting toward the baseline and toward the middle before releasing the ball off the backboard.

Offensive-Defensive Exchange

Players pair off along the end line. One player has the ball standing on the end line and facing downcourt. The partner is standing five feet in front facing so they are looking at each other (Diagram 3-3).

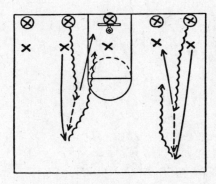

Diagram 3-3

On command, the players with a basketball start dribbling forward. Their partners meanwhile start back pedaling down the floor maintaining proper distance and spacing. On a whistle, the dribblers toss the ball forward to the partners who immediately stop back pedaling and start dribbling forward. Roles are reversed and partners exchange dribbling and back pedaling. Each time the whistle is sounded, partners reverse directions of the ball. Changing direction with dribbling forward and back pedaling continues for a one-minute period or until the dribbler can move close enough to touch the defender.

AMBIDEXTERITY

Ambidexterity is the ability to use either hand with equal dexterity or skill in developing a greater range of options and more possible alternatives in response selection.

Nonpreferred One-on-One

The players pair off according to size, ability, or position at a basket. A one-on-one game is played for a specified time period. All games start and finish together. The following restrictions are employed. A free throw shoot-off is used to determine who receives the ball on offense to start the competition. All dribbling is done with the nonpreferred hand. One dribble with the strong hand may be allowed to maintain control. The first shot on offensive possession must be taken with the nonpreferred hand. The player scoring retains possession on offense. The ball must be brought behind the free throw line on a change of possession.

Weak-Hand Shooting

The players pair off according to size, ability, or position at a basket. The same rules outlined in the previous drill are used except that all shooting attempts are taken with the nonpreferred hand.

Weak-Hand Passing

Using size and ability factors, the squad is divided into teams of three. A game of three-on-three is played. A free throw shoot-off determines which team receives the ball to start the game. The team scoring retains possession. The ball must be taken behind the free throw line on a change of possession. All passing must be done with the nonpreferred hand. (Two-hand chest-overhead-bounce passes are not allowed.)

KINESTHESIS (MUSCLE AWARENESS)

Kinesthesis is a sense of what muscles are doing in the performance of a skill. A sense of "feel" or awareness is essential in developing muscle memory to aid learning and execution of skills.

Eyes Closed

All players have a ball and are assigned to a basket. Developing a sense of "feel" for various skills is primary to developing muscle awareness. An important technique to use in attempting to develop the "feel" as well as proper movement is to close the eyes in performing different skills. The following list of maneuvers will help in establishing movement patterns as well as developing a sense of how the successful execution of the skill will feel.

1. Perform dribbling maneuvers in place (low dribble—high dribble— fast dribble—slow dribble—forward three dribbles—backward three dribbles—slide right three dribbles—slide left three dribbles— crossover dribble in place—reverse or spin dribble—continuous alternating left and right dribbling—behind the back dribble— through the legs dribble).
2. Practice the shooting release, follow through, and the full extension of the shot against a wall.
3. Shoot right- and left-handed layups off the backboard.
4. Shoot free throws.
5. Pass the ball off the wall.
6. Practice correct jumping technique (step-gather-release).
7. Practice running in place.
8. Practice pivoting techniques.
9. Practice correct lateral sliding techniques.

ANTICIPATION

Anticipation is the ability to recognize specific cues and make appropriate responses as quickly as possible. This enables players to

gain an advantage in executing the next skill to counteract the
opponent's plan of attack. The best method to develop or improve
anticipation is model training. This involves exposing players to as
many game situations as possible in practice to develop the appropriate actions or reactions necessary to succeed. By incorporating a
variety of drills in practice, players will be exposed to many potential
situations. This also helps to reduce the stress and tension that often
happens when a player is confronted with a game situation that was
not covered in practice. It is extremely important that you verbally
analyze and evaluate situations where players correctly or incorrectly
react to a situation.

4
Improving dribbling skills and techniques

Through the years there have been many innovations in the game of basketball. Offensive and defensive systems as well as many varying philosophies have had a great impact in designing and implementing a variety of styles of play. However, throughout all these changes the game is still played with one basketball and the overall objective is still to score more points than the opposition. There are no ties; regardless of whether a team is offensively minded or defensively oriented, the team that scores more points wins. The primary objective is to gain possession of the ball and maintain control until a basket is scored. Because of the value of ball possession, it is imperative that each player develop skills to maintain control by dribbling and expert ball handling.

Certain players will handle the ball more often than others, but all players will eventually have possession of the ball at some time during the game. Therefore, it is essential that every player develop dribbling skills.

Many factors must be taken into consideration when outlining a program to develop dribbling techniques. Dribbling proficiency encompasses the following: the ability to dribble with speed; control; maneuverability to escape defenses; ability to penetrate defenses to develop scoring opportunities; ability to drive past a defender; ability to dribble equally well with both hands; and developing anticipation to know when and when not to dribble. Dribbling must be practiced until the ball becomes an extension of the hand.

SINGLE BALL DRIBBLING SERIES

There are many skill areas to be considered in developing dribbling proficiency. Concentration, control, and confidence are key factors in learning the various dribbling maneuvers. Isolating techniques and emphasizing specific aspects will help your players become more versatile dribblers.

Leg Scissors Exchange

Players spread out in random formation with a ball. They stand in a forward-back staggered position with the left leg in advance of the right. The ball is in the right hand. A dribble is executed from the right hand through the legs to the left. As soon as the ball reaches the left hand, the legs are switched in a scissors fashion with the right leg moving ahead of the left. The ball is then dribbled back through the legs to the right. The alternate dribbling and leg switching continues for a specified period of time. As the skill level and confidence increases, the spread of dribbling and switching increases until the players are executing as quickly as possible under control.

Variations: Players execute the same drill while wearing gloves.
Another variation is for players to use blinders while executing the drill.
A third variation is for the players to advance the ball down the floor while executing the drill.

Seesaw Motion

Players spread out in random formation with a basketball and stand in a side straddle position with the feet parallel. The ball is in the right hand in front of the body. With the right hand only, the ball is dribbled back and forth through the legs. The right hand must be switched quickly from front to back to maintain control. After a period of time, the dribbling motion continues with the left hand only from front to back. Emphasize developing a steady rhythm to the back and forth dribbling motion.

Variations: Players wear gloves while executing the drill.
Another variation is for the players to pair off and alternate turns dribbling two basketballs. One ball is dribbled in place to

the side of the body. At the same time, the other ball is dribbled back and forth through the legs in the previously described fashion.

Dead Ball Start

Players spread out and a ball is placed on the floor in front of them. They bend at the waist and flex the knees while placing one hand on the ball. With a quick slapping motion the players start the ball bouncing until they are dribbling in an upright position. Three dribbles are started with the right hand and then the left hand. After proficiency has been achieved, players attempt to start two balls dribbling simultaneously. If the players have difficulty in starting a dribble, they should try starting it with the heel of the hand or side of the fist.

Isolation Dribbling

Players spread out in random formation with a ball. They develop a feel for the basketball by executing a variety of isolated dribbling maneuvers involving various parts of the hand. The following skills are performed with both the left and right hands in place:

1. Control dribbling with the individual fingers.
2. Control dribbling with the side, back, and heel of the hand.
3. Players pair off and alternate turns dribbling two basketballs simultaneously.
4. Players execute these dribbling techniques with the eyes closed.
5. Players execute the dribbling techniques while moving forward, backward, and laterally left and right.

Full-Court Maneuvering

Players line up two deep on the end line. Partners alternate turns executing the following dribbling maneuvers going the full length of the court and back:

1. Dribbling forward with the ball below knees and slightly to the side for control.
2. Dribbling forward with the ball above the waist and pushed out in front of the body to emphasize speed.
3. Dribbling backwards for control.

4. Slide dribbling laterally to the left and right for control. When sliding to the left, the ball is dribbled with the right hand. When sliding to the right, the ball is dribbled with the left hand.

5. Dribbling forward with a stop-and-go action emphasizing acceleration on starting and maintaining balance when stopping. Three dribbles are used to accelerate followed by two dribbles in place while stopping.

6. Dribbling forward utilizing a crossover technique. The ball is dribbled forward three dribbles with the right hand and then crossed over to the left. The same procedure is followed with the left-hand start and crossing over to the right.

7. Dribbling forward and executing a reverse or spin dribble each time three dribbles have been completed.

8. Dribbling forward while executing a through-the-legs transfer of the ball to the opposite hand. Start dribbling with the right hand. After three dribbles have been completed, the left leg is leading and the ball is dribbled between the legs to the left hand. Three more dribbles forward and the ball is transferred back to the right hand between the legs. The same procedure is followed full court and back.

9. Dribbling forward while executing a behind-the-back dribble. After every three dribbles forward, the ball is transferred to the other hand by dribbling behind the back.

Variations: Players execute the above dribbling maneuvers while wearing gloves.

Players execute the maneuvers while wearing blinders.

Dribble Change Series

The players line up single file behind the end line with a basketball (Diagram 4-1). The first player in line starts dribbling with the right hand to the free throw line. The ball is crossed over to the left with a stop-and-go maneuver. The ball is dribbled with the left hand to the juncture of the sideline and midcourt line. At that point a reverse or spin dribble is executed. After transferring to the right hand, the ball is dribbled to the top of the free throw circle. At this point the ball is dribbled through the legs back to the left hand and continued toward the left corner. After three or four dribbles, the ball is dribbled behind the back from left to right to change direction. The ball is then dribbled to the basket for a layup. All maneuvers are executed at the established points with concentration on quick

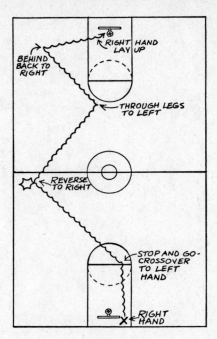

Diagram 4-1

acceleration to the next area of change. As soon as the first player has crossed half court, the next player in line starts to dribble. After each player has completed the series several times starting with the right hand, the same is done starting with the left hand.

Variation: Assign players to each dribble change spot to offer token defense as offensive players execute maneuvers.

Hopping and Dribbling

Players spread out along the end line with a ball. On command, all players together dribble the length of the court and back executing the following maneuvers:

1. Hopping on the right foot and dribbling with the right hand.
2. Hopping on the left foot and dribbling with the left hand.
3. Hopping on the right foot and dribbling with the left hand.
4. Hopping on the left foot and dribbling with the right hand.
5. Hopping with both feet together while alternating dribbling with the left and right hands.

Variations: The dribbling maneuvers are performed while hopping backward.

Another variation is to perform the dribbling maneuvers while hopping laterally to the right and left.

DOUBLE DRIBBLING SERIES

Dribble control can be improved by dribbling two basketballs at the same time. By increasing the difficulty to concentrate, the players must react to touch and feel to develop an awareness of ball and hand position in executing dribbling techniques. Consequently, habit formation replaces conscious effort in the execution of the skill.

Same Height

Players pair off with two basketballs on the end line. Partners alternate turns dribbling two balls at the same time and concentrate on keeping both balls at the same height while:

1. Walking and dribbling at waist level the length of the court and back.
2. Dribbling below the waist while hopping a length and back.
3. Dribbling above the waist while running a length and back.
4. Dribbling above the waist while striding a length and back.
5. Dribbling above the waist while galloping a length and back.
6. Dribbling above the waist while skipping a length and back.
7. Walking backward while dribbling at waist level.
8. Jogging backward while dribbling at waist level.
9. Sliding to the right while dribbling at waist level.
10. Sliding to the left while dribbling at waist level.
11. Hopping on the left foot while dribbling at waist level.
12. Hopping on the right foot while dribbling at waist level.
13. Hopping on both feet while dribbling at waist level.

High-Low Dribble

Players pair off with two balls on the end line. Partners alternate turns dribbling the two balls. One basketball is dribbled above the waist and the other below the waist when performing the following dribbling maneuvers:

1. Walking and dribbling a length of the court and back.
2. Jogging a length of the court and back.
3. Galloping a length of the court and back.
4. Skipping a length of the court and back.
5. Walking backward a length and back.
6. Sliding to the right a length and back. The right hand is high and the left hand is low while dribbling.
7. Sliding to the left a length and back. The left hand is high and the right hand is low while dribbling.
8. Hopping on the left foot a length and back. The left-hand dribble is low and the right-hand dribble is high.
9. Hopping on the right foot a length and back. The right-hand dribble is low and the left hand dribble is high.
10. Hopping on both feet a length and back.

Wall Dribble

Players pair off with two balls and face a wall. Partners alternate turns dribbling two balls off the wall. A ten-second time period is used as the following dribbling techniques are used:

1. Both balls are dribbled at shoulder level.
2. Both balls are dribbled above the head.
3. Both balls are dribbled at shoulder level outside the width of the body.
4. With fingers pointed down, both balls are dribbled off the wall below the waist.

Variations: The balls are dribbled simultaneously off the wall in the various positions described.

Another variation is to dribble the balls in an alternating rhythm in the various positions.

Wall-Floor Dribble

Players pair off with two basketballs and face a wall. Partners alternate turns dribbling both basketballs for ten-second time periods. On a signal, the following sequence of dribbling skills are performed:

1. Left hand dribbles off the wall and right hand dribbles off the floor above the waist.
2. Right hand dribbles off the wall and left hand dribbles off the floor above the waist.

3. With the left shoulder facing the wall, the left hand dribbles off the wall and the right hand dribbles off the floor below the waist.

4. With the right shoulder facing the wall, the right hand dribbles off the wall and the left hand dribbles off the floor below the waist.

Variations: The basketballs are dribbled simultaneously off the wall and the floor.

Another variation is to dribble the balls in an alternating rhythm off the wall and floor.

DRIBBLING MANEUVERABILITY

The ability to maneuver in different directions at varying speeds using many dribbling skills is essential to becoming an effective offensive threat. The ability to execute a variety of techniques efficiently gives the advantage to the offensive player.

Dribble Square

Divide the squad in half. Both groups spread out and face each other on opposite sides of the half-court line with a basketball (Diagram 4-2).

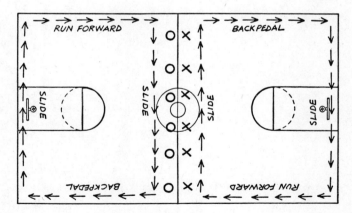

Diagram 4-2

Each group starts sliding and dribbling in a clockwise direction on their half-court area. When the players reach the juncture of the sideline and half-court line, they back pedal and dribble down the sideline until they reach the end line. They slide and dribble to the left across the end line. Upon reaching the juncture of the end line and sideline, they run forward and dribble back to the half-court line.

The same dribbling sequence around half court is continued for one minute. When time is up, the dribbling direction is reversed (counterclockwise) and the same dribbling procedures are followed. Emphasize keeping the eyes up at all times while controlling the ball and changing direction around the court. The tempo of the drill may be increased or decreased depending upon the skill level of the players.

Variations: Assign the players a partner from the other group. Every time they pass each other going in the opposite direction at half court, they exchange basketballs. One side throws a bounce pass while the other side throws a chest pass.

Another variation is for the players to spread out equidistant around their half-court area. As the drill proceeds, basketballs are exchanged every time someone is passed from the other group at the half-court line.

Dribble Steal

Players pair off with the groups spread out on the court. Each player has a basketball and faces the partner in dribbling position. On a signal, each partner starts dribbling a basketball and attempts to steal or deflect the partner's ball.

The following restrictions are employed:

1. Partners must face each other at all times while dribbling and stealing.
2. Kicking the ball is not allowed.
3. No physical contact is allowed other than occasional bumping or hand movement.

Variations: Players dribble with the right hand only and use the left hand to deflect or steal partner's basketball.

A second variation is for the players to dribble with the left hand only and use the right hand to deflect or steal the partner's basketball.

A third variation is to allow the players to dribble with either hand while using the free hand to steal the ball.

A fourth variation is to place players in groups of three and execute dribble and steal techniques.

A time period of thirty seconds is used with a brief rest period before starting again.

Circle Dribble

Divide the squad into two groups. Assign each group to opposite ends of the court. Every player has a basketball (Diagram 4-3).

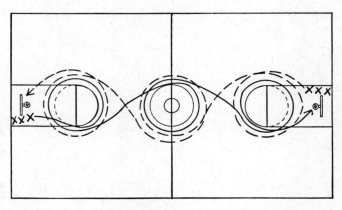

Diagram 4-3

On your signal, the first player in each group starts dribbling with the right hand around the free throw circle. After the circle is completed, the player dribbles toward the center circle with the left hand and completes a circle. The next task is to proceed to the opposite free throw circle crossing the ball back to the right hand and completing a circle before making a layup. Players then move to the end of the line. Both groups are moving at the same time and players must be alert to avoid contact as they pass each other going in the opposite direction around the circles. As soon as the first player in line completes a turn around the free throw circle, the next player begins. There will always be six to eight players dribbling the course at the same time.

Variations: Players start dribbling with the right hand from one end and with the left hand when returning from the other end.

Another variation is to have the players use different changeover dribbling techniques when moving from one circle to the next including a crossover, reverse or spin, behind the back, and through the legs.

Dribble Tag

Players spread out in random formation with a basketball. Players must stay within the court boundary lines (end lines and sidelines). Everyone starts dribbling anywhere within the boundary lines. Designate one player as "It" to start the drill. This person attempts to hand tag someone while all players dribble away to escape. The player tagged becomes "It." The following restrictions are imposed for the drill:

1. If a player dribbles outside the boundary line, that player is automatically "It."
2. A player cannot tag the same person twice.
3. Players cannot retag each other.
4. Players dribble with the right hand only, left hand only, or use either hand in pursuit.

Variations: Tag is played with one less basketball than the number of players involved. "It" does not have a ball to dribble allowing that person to move faster to get someone.

Another variation is for players to hop and dribble while playing tag.

A final variation is not allowing players more than three consecutive dribbles with the same hand.

Dribble Elimination

Players spread out in random formation with a ball. They must stay within the half-court area bounded by sidelines, end line, and half-court line. On your signal, all players start dribbling and moving inside the half-court area. The object is to protect and control a basketball while at the same time attempting to knock any other player's ball outside the boundary lines. When the time limit is up, the players remaining stop and rest. The eliminated players go to the end line and are assessed sprints.

Variations: Players are assigned to groups of four and play an elimination game inside a foul lane (area bordered by end line, foul lanes, and foul line) at a designated basket.

Another variation is to assign players in groups of three and play an elimination game inside a jump circle at a basket.

Dribble Keep Away

Divide the squad into groups of three and assign to a free throw lane. Each group has one basketball. On your signal, one player in each group starts dribbling a basketball. The remaining two players attempt to accomplish one of three objectives during the twenty-second time period:

1. Force the dribbler to stop dribbling and pick up the ball.
2. Steal the ball cleanly without fouling.
3. Deflect the ball outside the lane without fouling the dribbler.

DRIBBLING AIDS

The use of specialized aids in developing dribbling skills provides the players with additional obstacles in developing individual proficiency. Utilizing aids puts an additional demand on the concentration of the players in their attempt to improve a specific skill to the highest degree possible within the confines of self-limitations. Aids also provide a change of pace from the daily routine as well as adding a new dimension in the perfection of a skill. Finally, aids can develop confidence and motivate players as they feel they are gaining an extra "edge."

Dribble Blinders

Players spread out in random formation with a basketball and a pair of dribble blinders. The following techniques are practiced on verbal command from you:

1. Dribbling below the knee with the right hand, left hand, and an alternating left-right exchange.
2. Dribbling above the knee with the right hand, left hand, and alternating left-right exchange.
3. Reverse spin dribble with the left and right hands.
4. Through the legs dribble from left to right and right to left.
5. Behind the back dribble from right to left and left to right.
6. Hopping on both feet and alternating left-right dribbling exchange.
7. Hopping on the left foot while dribbling with the left hand and then the right.
8. Hopping on the right foot while dribbling with the right hand and then the left.

Dribbling with Gloves

Players spread out along the end line with a basketball and wearing a pair of gloves. On command, the players execute the following dribbling maneuvers while wearing the gloves:

1. Full-court running forward while dribbling above the waist and then below on the way back.
2. Full-court skipping and dribbling.
3. Full-court galloping and dribbling.
4. Full-court sliding and dribbling with both the right and left hands.
5. Full-court dribbling backward with the ball above the waist and below the waist on the way back.

Variation: After proficiency has been developed, players dribble two balls using the same sequence. In addition, a high-low dribbling technique which was explained earlier is used.

Blinders and gloves can also be used in many other practice areas. They are very effective aids in drills for passing, shooting, rebounding, and fast breaks. They can also be beneficial under controlled scrimmage conditions. Such situations include out-of-bounds plays, jump ball matchups, press work, free throw rebounding, and half-court scrimmage work.

Dribbling Kinesthesis

Players spread out in random formation with a basketball. They are directed to perform stationary dribbling skills. They include dribbling below the knee, above the knee, spin or reverse maneuvers, running and dribbling in place, figure-eight dribbling, alternating left and right in front of the body, behind the back dribbling, and through the legs dribbling. After the dribbling is in progress, signal to the players to close their eyes while continuing the dribbling. The purpose is to develop rhythm, tempo, and a sense of feel through various hand pressures exerted to perform the drill.

Closing the eyes is extremely helpful in working on shooting accuracy. Players learn to develop a muscle feel on release, which will aid in developing shooting consistency. Players work on their release around the basket, layups off the backboard, short hook shots, and free throw shooting by closing the eyes at the moment of release.

5
Improving ball-handling skills and techniques

The art of ball handling implies the ability to control the ball with sure-handedness. Many times a split second is the difference between maintaining possession, losing possession by fumbling, being unable to deliver the ball to an open teammate, or having the ball stolen by the defense.

The development of hand strength is important in being able to maintain possession and protect the basketball. In addition, ball-handling ability involves development in the area of catching a ball; holding the ball securely in an offensive threat position; passing the ball crisply; preparing to drive or dribble to initiate offensive movement; moving the ball into position to shoot; protecting the ball after the dribble is used; and sensing position of the ball so that control may be gained quickly when the ball is loose around the body or on the floor. The following drills in this chapter will aid in developing the necessary ball-handling skills that are essential in gaining and maintaining possession of the basketball.

HAND STRENGTH

Developing hand strength is vital to developing fingertip control and better hands in passing and receiving a basketball. It is necessary to utilize exercises specifically designed to develop finger, hand, and wrist strength.

Squeeze-Release

Each player performs a series of maneuvers with a basketball. The movements are designed to strengthen wrists and fingers in addition to developing a "touch" for the ball.

1. The ball is held in the fingertips below the knee. On command, the ball is squeezed for five seconds. A five-second rest period follows. The exercise is repeated three times.
2. The ball is held at the waist level while alternating squeezing and relaxing for five-second periods.
3. The ball is held overhead and the same procedures previously outlined are followed.
4. The ball is held behind the back and the same routine is followed.
5. The ball is held between the legs with one hand in front of the body and one hand behind the back following the same technique of squeezing and relaxing for a five-second interval.

Ball Pickup

Players spread out with a ball. The ball is placed on the floor in front of the feet. The right hand is placed on top of the ball with the fingers spread wide. On your whistle, players exert downward pressure on the ball and continue for three seconds. On a second whistle after the time is up, players reverse pressure and attempt to pick the ball off the floor with one hand. The exercise is repeated three times. The left hand is then placed on top of the basketball and the same procedure of pressing and lifting is performed.

Variation: Players work in pairs. One partner attempts to execute the drill with two basketballs simultaneously. Partners alternate turns.

Ball Slam

Players spread out and hold a ball in front of the body with feet shoulder width apart. The drill starts with the ball being held at knee level. On a signal from you, players slam the ball as hard as possible to the floor and catch at knee level. Players continue slamming and catching the ball as fast as possible for five seconds. The ball is then held at waist level and the same drill continued.

Variation: The eyes are closed while the ball is being slammed and caught.

Finger-Wrist Flick

Players spread out and face a wall at a distance of four feet. They bend at the waist with their knees flexed and the hands are held below the knee with the palms up. On a signal from you, the ball is bounced low off the wall using fingertip control in a flicking fashion with the wrist. Players tap the ball continuously off the wall. The sequence is for the ball to hit the wall, bounce off the floor in front of the knees, and be contacted on the rebound by the players who then flick the ball back against the wall. The fingers are pointed downward during the flicking action. The drill is performed with the right hand for ten seconds. The left hand is used for the next ten-second period. The third set is for both hands to be used alternately. Once consistent control is developed with one-hand control, two balls are flicked simultaneously with players pairing off and alternating turns with partners.

Fingertip Pushups

There are three fingertip pushup exercises used to develop strength in the fingers, hands, forearms, and wrists. The first exercise starts with the players facing a wall and standing arms-length away. The fingers are cupped and placed on the wall in a full-arm extension position. The elbows are bent until the nose touches the wall. On the push back to a full-arm extension, the movement is a quick explosive thrust. These pushups are executed ten times. During the exercise, the feet are flat on the floor and the back is straight to place full emphasis on arm extension. The second exercise involves the players lying on the floor in a prone position. The arms are extended in a straight-arm support position with the back straight and the weight supported entirely on the fingertips and toes. On command, the body is lowered to the floor until the chin touches. This is followed by a quick explosive thrust back to the full-arm extension position. The pushups are executed in the same fashion concentrating on a slow recovery and quick extension. The third pushup exercise involves the players placing both hands on a basketball and supporting their weight on the hands and toes in a full-arm extended position on the floor. One or two basketballs may be used. Keeping the back straight, players lower themselves to the floor slowly and as low as possible. With an explosive thrust, players return to a full-arm extended position.

Pull Ball Away

Players pair off with one ball and face each other. The ball is held between them in a full-arm extension. One player has the hands positioned on the sides of the ball. The partner has the hands on the top and bottom of the ball. The ball is held by the fingertips of both players. On a whistle from you, the players react and attempt to gain possession of the ball by pulling toward themselves with a quick movement using the arms only. Feet remain flat on the floor in a parallel position. Loss of the ball or shifting of the feet ends the contest. Players reset their positions for the next contest. After three chances for possession, players reverse hand positions on the ball and wait for the next whistle to continue the drill.

Push Ball Away

Players pair off with one ball and face each other. The ball is positioned between them at chest level. One player holds the ball with the hands on the side of the ball while the partner's hands are on the top and bottom of the ball. Their feet are opposite each other and parallel. They stand close enough so that elbows are bent at a right angle while holding the ball. On a whistle, both players react as quickly as possible to the sound and push the ball to a full-arm extended position. They attempt to force the other player off-balance. After the contest is over, players reset themselves with the hands in the same position and wait for the next whistle. After three chances, players switch hand positions on the ball. Both the pull-away and push-away competition can be organized into a single elimination tournament.

Knock Ball Loose

Players pair off with one ball. One player holds the ball in front of the chest with hands on the side of the ball. Elbows are bent at a right angle. The partner makes a fist with both hands and positions them six inches above and below the ball. On a whistle, an attempt is made to knock the ball loose with either a quick downward or upward pop with the fist or heel of the hand. Each player gets three chances as holder while the partner attempts to knock the ball loose. Restrictions include:

1. The player attempting to knock the ball loose must hit only once in a single direction (up or down) each time the whistle is sounded.
2. The hands must always remain at a distance not exceeding six inches on the top or bottom of the ball.
3. The player holding the ball must make sure the ball is away from the face to prevent possible injury if the ball is knocked loose on the upward thrust. The weight is kept back on the heels and the head is tilted slightly back.

BALL MOVEMENT

In order to develop a feel for the basketball and a sense of control, a program of ball-related drills based on movement must be incorporated. Accuracy, hand-eye coordination, control, and ball awareness can be developed by isolating specific skills designed to increase the touch and fingertip control of the ball. Rapid movement of the ball around different areas of the body will help accomplish these objectives.

In and Out

Players spread out in random formation with a ball. They stand with feet shoulder width apart. The ball is started around the outside of the right leg with the right hand while players are bent around the waist. The left hand continues the motion by picking up the ball from the right hand as it passes between the legs. The left hand continues with the ball to the outside of the left leg and between the legs back to the right hand. The same continuous sequence of ball movement in a figure-eight manner continues as quickly as possible for ten seconds.

Variations: The ball is started with the right hand pushing the ball between the legs from in front and picked up by the left hand from behind. The left hand travels forward outside the left leg to be pushed through the legs from the front. The rapid movement continues for ten seconds. The ball is moved around the legs below the knees for ten seconds and then above the knees for ten seconds.

A second variation is to reverse the direction of the ball each time a figure eight is completed. This is done first below the knees for a period of time and then above the knees.

A third variation is to drop the ball to the floor and recover it before reversing direction after a figure eight is completed.

Body Circle

Players spread out in random formation with a basketball. They stand with their feet together. The ball is held below the knees in front of the body. On command, the ball is moved around the legs in a clockwise direction as fast as possible five times. After completion, the ball is reversed to a counterclockwise direction for five circles. This sequence continues until direction is reversed three times.

Variations: The ball is circled around the legs at the knee level and reversed after five times.

A second variation is moving the ball around the waist five times reversing.

A third variation is moving the ball around the head and reversing.

Self-Catch

Players spread out with a ball. They stand erect with their feet far enough apart to allow the basketball to pass between the legs. The ball is held with both hands out in front of the body. On a signal, the ball is bounced between the legs. The hands are moved behind the body to recatch the ball. When caught, the ball is bounced back through the legs and caught again in front. The back and forth self-passing continues with the tempo increasing as proficiency is achieved.

Variations: The ball is slammed as hard as possible from front to back through the legs. The ball is brought around to the front of the body again in a quick half-circle and slammed through the legs again. Each time the ball is caught behind, the ball is brought to the front of the body in the opposite direction.

A second variation is to pass the ball from back to front through the legs. When caught, the ball is moved in a half-circle to the back before passing through the legs again.

Hand-Hand Flip Control

Players spread out with a ball. They stand with the feet comfortably apart. The ball is held in and controlled with the fingertips only. The ball is positioned so that it may be flipped rapidly back and forth from hand to hand. The hands are twelve to sixteen inches apart. There are eight areas where this quick exchange takes place:

1. Over the top of the sneakers.
2. In front of the knees.
3. In front of the waist.
4. In front of the shoulders.
5. Overhead.
6. Behind the back and above the buttocks.
7. Behind the knees.
8. Between the legs with one hand in front and behind.

HAND-EYE COORDINATION DEVELOPMENT

A key to accuracy in shooting and passing, control in dribbling, and timing in rebounding is development in hand-eye coordination. This can be aided by concentrating on drills that will isolate this concept and afford practice on locating and recatching the ball.

Back to Wall Catch

Each player has a ball and stands with the back to the wall about eight to ten feet away. Feet are shoulder width apart. The ball is bounced through the legs so it will rebound off the wall after bouncing off the floor. After the ball makes contact with the floor, players jump-turn to the left or right to face the wall. They locate and catch it before it hits the floor again. Distance from the wall and speed of the throw are varied to increase the awareness to locate and catch the ball after the jump turn.

Variations: Players execute the same drill but receive the ball with one hand only.

A second variation is to bounce the ball through the legs at an angle that will carry the ball off the wall and overhead. Without turning, players locate the ball by looking straight back overhead and then catch the ball before it hits the floor in front of the body.

Continuous Shoulder Toss

Players spread out with a basketball and stand erect in a comfortable stance. The ball is balanced on the right hand out in front of the body with the palm up. The ball is then reversed with right-hand control only by turning the hand inside between the arm and body. From this position the ball is flipped up and over the left shoulder from behind the back and caught with the left hand only in front of the body. As soon as control is established, the left hand reverses between the arm and body to flip the ball over the right shoulder from behind the back. This figure-eight flipping action over the shoulder from left to right and back continues as quickly as possible. Concentration is always on establishing one-hand control on reception and moving immediately to a passing position.

Variation: Players pair off with two balls. Partners alternate turns with one player using both balls to execute the drill. Both balls are supported in front of the body with the palms up. The drill starts with one basketball tossed over the opposite shoulder from behind the back. The other ball shifts quickly to the free hand in front of the body to allow for a one-hand reception of the ball coming over the shoulder. After continuing in the same direction for several passes, the direction reverses to allow for opposite hand reception.

Catch Behind Back

Players spread out with a ball with plenty of room to perform this drill to eliminate any possibility of injury. The players stand erect holding the ball in front of the body. They toss the ball up and over the head to catch the ball with the hands behind the back. On each succeeding toss, the ball is thrown higher. Eventually, the ball is tossed as high as possible with the players circling under the ball to catch it behind the back.

Variations: After the toss, players make a quarter-, half-, or three-quarter turn before catching the ball behind the back.

A second variation is to have the players count the number of times they can clap the hands in front and back of the body before catching the ball behind the back.

A third variation is for the players to toss the ball forward or to either side and move in that direction to reestablish position and catch the ball behind the back.

A final variation is for players to work in pairs and toss the ball in the air for each other to catch behind the back.

Back and Over Catch

Players spread out and stand erect in a comfortable stance while holding a ball behind the back. The ball is tossed up and over the head from behind to the front of the body. The first few times the players are allowed to tilt the head back to catch the ball as it passes over the head. As proficiency improves, the second phase is for the players to keep the head stationary and only roll the eyes upward to sight the ball and catch it. The last stage is for the players to keep the head stationary and look straight ahead. They locate and catch the ball as it passes through their range of vision in front of the face.

Variations: Players use a one-hand reception in catching the ball. They alternate hands on each catch.

A second variation is for players who have difficulty resisting the urge to look up for the ball; they use dribble blinders placed above the eyes on the forehead.

HAND SPEED

Hand speed is the ability to move the hands as quickly as possible in a coordinated movement to accomplish the goal of receiving, releasing, and changing position of the ball without losing control or balance. Fingertip control, knowledge of hand position, and hand-eye coordination are essential to developing and improving hand speed.

Release-Reverse-Recatch

Players spread out with a ball and take a stance with their legs shoulder width apart and feet parallel. Players bend at the waist with the ball held between the legs; the left hand is in front of the body and right hand is behind. On your signal, players release the ball, reverse the hands, and recatch the ball before it hits the floor. The right hand is now in front and the left hand behind. The continuous reversing of the hands and recatching the ball is accomplished as fast as possible for ten seconds. Three sets of the drill are completed with a ten-second rest interval between.

Variation: The ball is held between the legs with both hands in front of the body and below the knees. The ball is released and both hands move behind the body to catch the ball. This front-back catching and releasing is done for ten-second intervals with a brief rest period in between.

Clap Hands Recover

Players spread out with a ball and stand erect with their feet comfortably apart. The object is to drop the basketball from different heights, clap the hands in front or behind the body, and recatch the ball before it hits the floor. Emphasize dropping the ball and not tossing it up before recovering. The ball is held in front of the face to start. On each drop and successful reception, the ball is moved to a lower position (chest-waist-thighs-knees-shins) before dropping. From all positions the hands are clapped behind the back before recatching. When the players have completed dropping the ball from all areas in front of the body, the ball is held behind the body and dropped. The hand clap occurs in front as the ball is dropped from the lower back area, buttocks, hamstrings, back of knees, and behind the calves.

Fingertip Flip

Players spread out with a ball and take a comfortable stance while bending at the waist and flexing the knees slightly. The ball is held and controlled by the fingertips. The first position in which the ball is held is just above the sneaker tops. On a signal from you, the ball is flipped back and forth from left to right with the hands apart approximately twelve inches. Each time the ball is flipped back and forth, the players gradually move the ball up the front of the body until a full arm extension above the head is reached. Once overhead, the drill continues with the ball being moved back down until it is back to the starting position. This procedure continues until the ball has made five trips up and down the body.

> **Variations:** When proficiency has been established, players close the eyes and perform the same movement pattern.
>
> A second variation is to hold the ball behind the body starting at the ankles. The ball is moved up and down as high as possible using the same techniques as in front of the body.

Ball Drop Touch

Players spread out with a ball and stand erect with feet shoulder width apart and knees slightly flexed. The ball is held with the arms extended straight out in front at shoulder level. You will verbally call out numbers from one to four. Each number represents a specific area of the body that must be touched when the ball is dropped. When number one is called, players drop the ball. They quickly touch the shoulders and recover the ball before it hits the floor. They return the ball to the original starting position. On number two, players touch the stomach before recatching. On number three, players touch the buttocks before recovering the ball. On number four, players touch the knees before recovering. The numbers are called rapidly and in random order. The purpose of the drill is to teach concentration while reacting with hand speed to touch different parts of the anatomy and to feel different body stresses in bending and stretching to recover the ball before it hits the floor. Emphasize that the arms must be kept straight. The ball is dropped, not tossed, when numbers are called.

PERIPHERAL VISION

An important consideration for improving basketball skill is in the area of expanding the range of vision. By incorporating drills designed to diffuse the focus of concentration, players will be better able to handle basketballs moving in or from different directions as well as developing a wider range of vision. This is essential in becoming a better passer and delivering the ball quickly to an open player. Focusing on a constant point while keeping the head stationary will enable a player to develop peripheral vision.

Two-Ball Catch

Players pair off with two balls. Partners alternate turns using both. One partner holds both balls out in front of the body with the elbows bent and palms up. Head and eyes are held in a stationary position. Both balls are thrown and caught simultaneously on the palms. Each succeeding toss is higher as confidence and skill of catching improves. The tossing and catching continues until the players fail to catch both balls at once.

Variations: The hands are held in line with the elbows and shoulders while tossing and catching.

A second variation is for the hands to be held outside the line of the elbows to spread the basketballs wider when tossing and catching.

A third variation is to position the hands as far apart as possible while performing the drill.

Two-Ball Bounce-Catch

Players pair off with two balls and alternate turns using both at the same time. One partner holds both basketballs on the palms, which are held out in front of the body with the elbows bent. The eyes are focused straight ahead on a stationary object. The head is also held in a stationary position. Both balls are tossed simultaneously and bounced off each other in a glancing blow so that the balls will rebound into the air. This action causes the basketballs to bounce wider and makes it more difficult to recover them together on the palms. As the players become more proficient in the technique, the balls are thrown harder, which will cause them to rebound wider and higher and increase the difficulty to recover. Partners work at their own pace and continue to expand their lateral range of vision by bouncing basketballs to rebound further apart. After five tosses, partners alternate turns.

Peripheral Passing

Divide players into groups of three. Give each group two basketballs. Players B and C stand twelve feet away from each other with both facing player A (Diagram 5-1). Players A and C have a

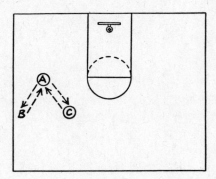

Diagram 5-1

basketball. Player A keeps the head stationary and focuses on a point straight ahead equidistant between players B and C. A passes to B and at the same time receives a pass from C. As soon as the ball is received, B passes back to A and A returns the pass to C. A is always concentrating on keeping the head stationary and looking straight ahead. After a thirty-second time period, players rotate positions. Bounce passes are thrown the first time through by the players. Second time around chest passes are thrown. Overhead passes are thrown the third time through the drill.

6
Improving passing and receiving techniques

The quickest way to advance the basketball up the floor and into scoring position is by passing. Passing is used to deliver the ball out of traffic on a rebound. Passing is the easiest and fastest method to defeat zone and player-to-player defensive pressure. Accurate passing is a must to get the ball inbounds. Passing is an art that is used in every phase of offensive basketball.

Passing and receiving a basketball requires a great deal of practice under varying conditions. These include two-, three-, and four-player exchange drills along with five-on-five scrimmage situations incorporating competitive and pressure conditions. This involves passing and receiving from stationary and moving positions.

There are many types of passes that must be developed for any defensive adjustment that might be encountered. They include the chest pass, bounce pass, overhead wrist pass, underhand flip pass, and baseball pass.

Hand speed for control along with developing peripheral vision are essential factors in improving the ability to pass and receive a basketball.

PASSING TECHNIQUES

Passing is essential in developing offensive scoring opportunities. Many techniques have to be learned and practiced to take advantage of the openings that will occur in a game. Passing to a stationary target, a target moving toward oneself, a target moving away, a target moving at an angle, and a target moving at varying speeds must be practiced. Repetition and concentration must be practiced to become an accurate and effective passer.

Moving and Passing Toward a Target

Divide the squad in half. Each line stands in single file facing the opposite line. The lines are fifteen to twenty feet apart (Diagram 6-1).

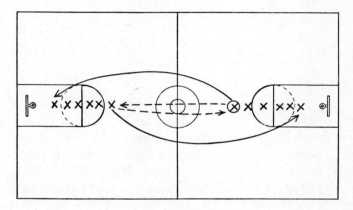

Diagram 6-1

One basketball is used in passing and receiving. The first player in line with the ball passes to the first player in the opposite line. After the pass is made, the player moves to the right and goes to the end of the opposite line. The receiver passes back to the other line and moves to the right going to the end of the other line. The drill is continuous as all players pass and go to the right to the end of the opposite line. After a period of time, you signal that all players move to the left after completing a pass. The following passing skills are executed on your command:

1. Chest Pass
2. Bounce Pass
3. Close Handoff
4. Behind Back Flip Pass
5. Scoop Pass-Off Dribble

Weave and Pass

Players line up in three lines along the end line (Diagram 6-2). The drill begins with B in the middle passing to either wing (A or C)

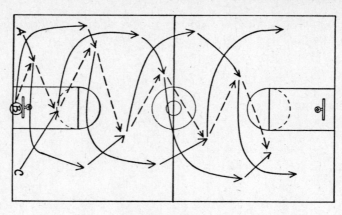

Diagram 6-2

and cutting behind to the outside and ahead. The player receiving the pass moves toward the middle of the floor and passes to the third player while cutting behind to the outside. Each time the ball is passed, the passer cuts behind the receiver to the sideline. This figure-eight movement pattern continues down the court and back with the following restrictions imposed to improve concentration and execution: The ball cannot touch the floor and no dribbling is allowed. The penalty for either infraction is continuing the drill until two consecutive lengths of the court are completed without dropping or dribbling the ball. Players rotate lines going from A to B to C after completing the drill.

Variations: A three-player weave is executed while making two layups in a row without the ball touching the floor.

A second variation is a four-player weave. The passer must cut behind and touch the sideline after passing before moving up-court. Three layups in a row must be made without the ball touching the floor.

Dribble Weave

The players line up on the end line in five lines evenly spaced apart (Diagram 6-3). Player A starts dribbling toward B and hands the ball off while cutting behind B and D and moving to the side line. Player B dribbles toward C and hands off while cutting behind C and E and moving to the sideline. Player C hands off to D; D hands off to E. Players continue dribbling, handing off, and cutting to touch the sideline before moving back toward the middle of the floor for another handoff. The groups of five must make four consecutive layups before moving off the court.

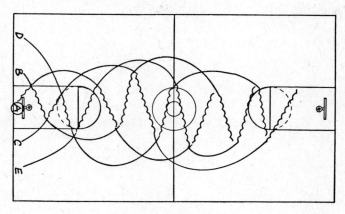

Diagram 6-3

Running and Passing

Divide the squad into four lines on the end line. Two lines working together are ten feet apart facing each other. Lines A and B pass together while C passes with D (Diagram 6-4). The first two in line start running downcourt passing a ball back and forth as quickly as possible. The goal is to complete six to eight passes moving downcourt and six to eight passes coming back. Each set of players

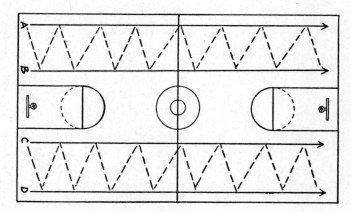

Diagram 6-4

takes three turns running and throwing a chest pass. The bounce pass is then thrown while running, followed by the overhead wrist pass to make nine trips for each set of players. Emphasize receiving and releasing the ball quickly with fingertip control.

Sliding and Passing

Divide players into four lines on the end line as in the previous drill. Two lines ten feet apart work together. The first two players start sliding laterally downcourt passing and receiving the ball back and forth as quickly as possible. The following types of passes are thrown with emphasis on fingertip control and quick release:

1. Chest Pass
2. Bounce Pass
3. Overhead Wrist Pass
4. Underhand Flip Pass

Variation: Each time a pass is received, the ball is quickly taken around the back and moved into position to pass back.

Zigzag Passing

Divide the squad evenly into two lines A and B. The lines spread out facing each other ten feet apart. Players in the same line are arm's length apart (Diagram 6-5). The first player in line A and B has a basketball. On your signal, player A throws a bounce pass to the first player to the left in line B. At the same time, player B throws a chest

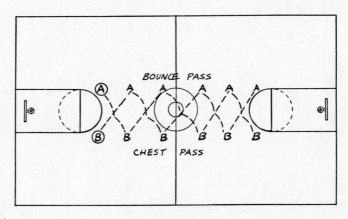

Diagram 6-5

pass to the first player on the right in line A. The two basketballs continue down the line passing over and under each other as line A throws bounce passes and line B throws chest passes. When the last two players in line receive the basketballs, they immediately reverse the direction of the ball with B throwing a chest pass and A throwing a bounce pass to start the balls back in the other direction. After several trips back and forth with the balls, on your command line A throws chest passes and line B throws bounce passes.

Variations: When both basketballs get to the last players in line, they immediately turn and dribble to the other end and start passing again. The drill is completed when the squad reaches the end of the court.

A second variation after proficiency has been achieved with two basketballs is to introduce four balls into the drill. Two start at the end and two start in the middle of the lines.

A third variation is to use six and possibly eight balls if the squad is large enough.

Passing Out Front

Divide the squad into groups of four. Two basketballs are used in each group. Three players in the group stand side by side six to eight feet apart. One player stands twelve to fifteen feet in front of the group facing them. On your signal, A passes to C while B passes to A. Immediatley upon receiving the pass, A passes to D and receives a pass from C. A passes to B and receives a pass from D. After thirty seconds, players switch positions with B moving out front and A replacing B in the line. Chest passes are thrown first. Bounce passes are thrown the second time around. Overhead passes are thrown the third time around.

Variations: Player A receives bounce passes and throws chest passes.

A second variation is for A to throw bounce passes and receive chest passes.

A third variation is for A to throw overhead passes and receive either chest or bounce passes.

Circle Passing

Divide the squad into groups of six. Five of the players form a circle with the sixth player assigned to the middle for defensive purposes. One ball is used. One player on the circle has the ball to start. The ball is passed back and forth across the circle involving all the players. The middle player attempts to touch, deflect, or intercept any pass that is thrown. Certain passing restrictions are imposed to improve concentration and accuracy. All passes must be made below the head level of the defender. The ball may not be passed to the next player on the immediate right or left. When the defender touches, deflects, or intercepts the ball, players switch positions. The defender moves to the outer circle. The player whose pass was deflected moves into the center on defense. A time limit may also be used to rotate players in and out of the middle position.

Variations: A circle of six players may be used to increase the number of available receivers from two to three on any pass thrown.

A second variation is for the entire squad to form a large circle. Two players are assigned to the inside of the circle on defense and two basketballs are passed.

Triangular Passing

Divide the squad into groups of three. They form a triangle ten feet apart from each other. One ball is used in each group. On a whistle from you, A passes to B, B passes to C, and C passes to A. The ball continues as fast as possible in a clockwise direction. Player A dictates the type of pass thrown; B and C must follow with the same pass. On your next whistle, the ball reverses direction and moves counterclockwise with A still determining the type of pass to be thrown. After one minute, allow a brief rest period. On the second series, B starts the passing and determines the type of pass thrown.

Perimeter Passing

Set up the squad in the five perimeter floor positions (left corner, left wing, top of key, right wing, right corner). Players line up two or three deep at each position. At least three must be at the point position (Diagram 6-6).

Two basketballs are used simultaneously. Player A at the point and E in the right corner have a basketball to start. On your whistle, both basketballs are passed. A passes to B and steps to the end of the line. E passes to C and steps back. B passs to D and C passes to A. The passing continues from point to wing to corner and back. Each time the ball is passed the passer steps back to the end of the line.

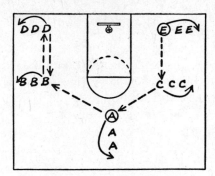

Diagram 6-6

Variations: Each time a player passes, that player then moves to the end of the same line to which the ball was passed.

A second variation is that each time a player passes, a move is made to the end of the line which is opposite the direction of the pass.

Pass-Exchange Drill

Set up the squad in a square formation with an equal number of players in each line. Two basketballs are used and start on opposite sides of the square. The following sequences of passing maneuvers are followed within the structure of the square:

1. Pass to the first person on the right and follow the pass to the outside end of the line.
2. Pass to the first person on the left and follow the pass to the outside end of the line.
3. Pass to the first person on the right and move to the end of the first line on the left.
4. Pass to the first person on the left and move to the end of the first line to the right.
5. Start both basketballs on the same side of the square.
   a. Pass to diagonal receiver and follow the pass to the end of the line.
   b. Pass to diagonal receiver and go to the end of the line on the right.
   c. Pass to diagonal receiver and go to the end of the line on the left.

The types of passes used are the chest, bounce, and overhead. Both balls are passed simultaneously and as quickly as possible after receiving them.

RECEIVING CONCENTRATION

The ability to receive a pass in balance from different positions and angles is necessary in becoming an offensive threat. Passes will vary in velocity and height. Passes will be received from stationary, advancing, retreating, and oblique targets. Receiving drills are necessary to develop the concentration of players to improve their ability to receive all types of passes, which often are poorly thrown and off target.

Up and Down

Divide players into two lines. Both lines start behind the end line and the width of the foul lane apart. Players work in pairs with one from each line passing together using one basketball. The first two in line start by sliding laterally downcourt facing each other. The ball is passed back and forth quickly starting with an overhead pass by each player. The second pass is a chest pass back and forth. The third pass is a bounce pass to each other at waist level. The fourth pass is an underhand flip pass at the knee level. The fifth pass is an underhand scoop pass as low as possible just over the sneaker tops. After the sequence is completed by sliding the length of the court, players turn and jog back to the end of the line. As soon as the first two players passing the ball cross half court, the next two in line start. Each time players finish a length, they return to the other line. This gives them an opportunity to slide both left and right in executing the drill.

Continuous Baseball Pass

Divide the squad into lines stationed at either end of the court outside the end line and near the side line (Diagram 6-7).

Each line has a basketball. One player from each line stands on the court opposite the free throw line. The first player in each line off the court has a basketball. Both lines start together on your signal by throwing a baseball pass to the player inbounds who is breaking downcourt. After the pass is received, the ball is dribbled down to the end line and out to the corner. The ball is then passed to the next player in line breaking deep; the passer moves to the end of the line. Players rotate from breaker to receiver to passer, and then to the end of the line. After several opportunities or a specific time limit, the drill is done with players streaking down the left side line.

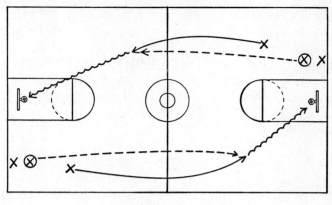

Diagram 6-7

Six Station Relay

Divide the squad into two groups. Group A is stationed at six designated spots on the court. Group B is lined up single file underneath a main basket with a basketball (Diagram 6-8).

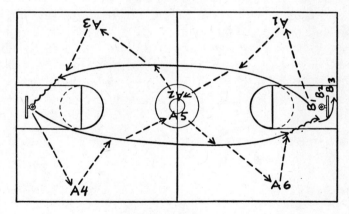

Diagram 6-8

Player B1 starts to the right and passes to A1 and receives the pass back while moving forward. B1 continues running and passes to A2 and gets the return pass. B1 continues running and passing in order to A3, A4, A5, and A6 each time receiving a pass back. B2 starts the circuit as soon as B1 receives a pass back from A1. Players continue running and passing for one minute. Groups A and B switch assignments. The second time through, players move to the left around the court passing and receiving the ball.

Variations: The entire group must run and pass for one minute without dropping or mishandling the ball. The penalty is a second consecutive minute.

A second variation is to shoot layups after receiving a pass back from positions 3 and 6 before continuing on the circuit. Every layup must be made during the one-minute time period.

Jumping and Passing

Players pair off in random formation around the court and stand ten to twelve feet apart. Each player has a basketball. On your signal, both partners start hopping in place. One partner throws a bounce pass and the other partner a chest pass as they exchange passes for thirty seconds. A ten-second rest period follows. Players then switch passes and start hopping and passing for thirty seconds again.

Establishing Control

Players spread out in random formation, each with a basketball. The drill starts by players dropping the basketballs to the floor. The drop is timed so that they pin the ball on the floor with the right hand just as the ball makes contact with the floor. This is accomplished three times with the right hand and three times with the left hand. After the technique of pinning the ball has been mastered, players start tossing the ball into the air before pinning on the floor with the left and right hand. The height of the toss is increased after each successful pin.

Variation: Players work in pairs. They toss the ball for each other alternating turns at pinning the ball.

Three and Two Drill

Divide the squad into three lines on the end line. Players in line A and B have a basketball (Diagram 6-9). The first player in each line starts runnning downcourt staying in their respective lane. Both basketballs are passed back and forth to the middle player B. B passes to C and turns to receive a pass from A. Upon reception, B passes quickly back to A and turns the head to receive a pass from C. The same procedure continues down the court and back with B passing and receiving both balls alternately. Players switch lines so that everyone has an opportunity to be in the middle position.

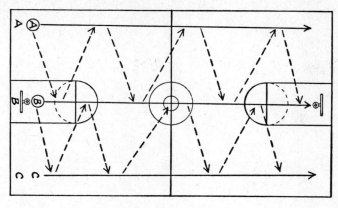

Diagram 6-9

Variations: Players must complete three consecutive lengths without letting either ball touch the floor.

A second variation is that the middle player must make two consecutive layups and rebound the ball before it hits the floor.

PASSING OFF TO THE OPEN PLAYER

The ability to pass off to a teammate after penetrating the defense is a valuable offensive asset. The art of receiving inside scoring opportunities rests upon the ability to penetrate on the dribble and pass off to an open player around the basket. Repeated practice is needed to give players the chance to react to defensive adjustments in the lane when penetrating toward the basket.

Block Drill

Divide the squad into guards and forwards. The guards have a ball and line up single file at half court. The forwards are out-of-bounds underneath the basket. The first two forwards step on the floor into the block position (first lane space) and face half court. Position yourself out-of-bounds under the basket in full view of the guards but in a position so the forwards cannot see your motions (Diagram 6-10).

The first guard in line starts driving straight down the middle of

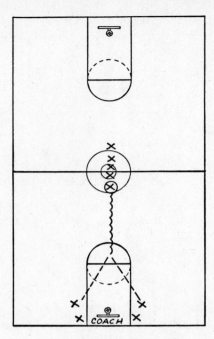

Diagram 6-10

the floor toward the basket with eyes up watching you. As the player approaches the top of the circle, you indicate with a hand signal which option the guard is going to complete. Point up if the guard is going to pull for a jump shot at the free throw line. Forwards turn, rebound, and tap in the missed shot. Point down if the guard is to drive all the way for a layup. Point to either forward. This indicates which forward will receive the bullet pass from the guard when reaching the top of the circle. Upon receiving the pass, the forward immediately pivots to the basket for a power layup off the backboard. As soon as the play is completed, the next guard starts to drive to the top of the circle to execute one of the options on your signal. Forwards always face the guard in a ready position to react to the appropriate situation.

Lane Reaction Drill

Divide the squad into groups of four. A has a basketball at half court. B and C stand in the first lane space on either side of the basket facing A. D plays defense standing in the middle of the lane on the bottom of the free throw circle and facing A (Diagram 6-11).

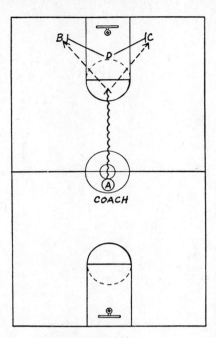

Diagram 6-11

Stand behind A at half court in plain view of the defensive player D. A starts driving toward the basket. Indicate by a hand signal to D which player (B or C) will be covered. When A touches the top of the circle, D moves to cover the player you designated. A must quickly pass to the open player for a layup.

Variation: Indicate to D to stay in the middle of the lane or to rush the dribbler; this forces A to diagnose more options upon driving toward the basket.

Read the Defense

Divide the squad into groups of five. A has a basketball at half court. B and C are positioned in the first lane space on either side of the basket. Groups 1 and 2 are defending B and C. You stand behind A at midcourt (Diagram 6-12). A starts driving toward the basket. Indicate which defensive player (1 or 2) will cover A at the top of the circle. A must pick out the open player and deliver a pass for a layup. Players rotate from A to 1 to B to 2 to C each time their group comes up.

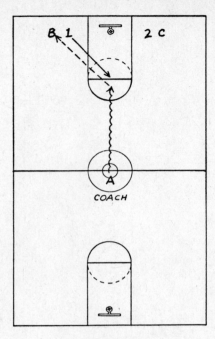

Diagram 6-12

INBOUNDS PASSING

The ability to execute and counteract defensive pressure starts with the skill of inbounding the ball successfully. Often the difference between accepting pressure or applying pressure rests in the hands of the inbounds passer.

Fronting Inbounds Receiver

Divide the squad into groups of three. A is the inbounds passer; B is the inbounds receiver; 1 is defensing B by fronting him. When players are in position, hand the ball to A and start a five-second count. B must get free and receive the pass inside the free throw line. No long passes are allowed. Players rotate from A to 1 to B before moving off for the next group.

Double Up Receiver

Divide the squad into groups of four. A is the inbounds passer. B is the receiver. Defenders 1 and 2 double up on B (Diagram 6-13).

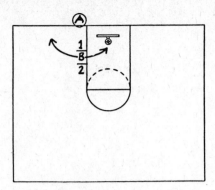

Diagram 6-13

After all four players are set, hand the ball to A and start a five-second hand count. B must make sharp movements to receive the ball inside the free throw line within the allotted time. On the first inbounds attempt, 1 and 2 play B side to side. Players rotate positions 1 to A to 2 to B each time their group comes on the floor.

Three on Two Inbounds

Divide the squad into groups of five. A is the inbounds passer. B is the inbounds receiver. Player 1 is defensing A on the end line; 2 and 3 are doubling up on B to prevent the pass inbounds. After all five players are set in their positions, hand the ball to A and start a five-second hand count. B makes quick movements to get free and receive the pass inbounds within the allotted time. After the ball is inbounds, players A and B have ten seconds to get the ball over half court as 1, 2, and 3 attempt to trap and stop the ball from advancing.

Variation: A is allowed to move back and forth along the end line to make the pass inbounds. B is also allowed to jump out-of-bounds to receive the pass and then pass back to A inbounds as long as the five-second count is not violated.

7
Improving shooting skills and techniques

The ability to score and put more points on the scoreboard than the opponent will ultimately determine the outcome of the game. Many skills are involved in developing shooting ability and scoring potential. Body balance, body position, proper alignment to the basket, proper elevation of the ball on release, proper backspin rotation, and full arm extension on the follow through are essential to the mechanics of shooting.

Developing a quick release, shooting from a stationary position, shooting off a dribble maneuver, and shooting in traffic where contact will occur are some of the many skills that have to be learned and practiced.

Shooting from different areas on the floor requires a great deal of concentration and practical application reinforced through isolated shooting drills.

Confidence is a primary factor in perfecting shooting skills and determining individual shooting range for effectiveness. The drills contained in this chapter are designed to place emphasis on the type of shots that will occur during a game along with developing the special techniques necessary for each player to become a better player.

ACCURACY

Accuracy or preciseness is a skill that must be emphasized in every phase of basketball, but especially shooting. Shooting skill will be improved by concentrating on the mechanical principles involved and constant reinforcement in practice through specific shooting drills.

Standing Release

Evenly divide the squad among the available baskets. Partners alternate shooting turns. One ball is used at each basket. Three shooting spots are designated around the basket. Players take five shots from each spot while standing with feet parallel and shoulders square to the basket. The spots are located six feet from the basket in front, on the left side in line with the rim, and on the right side of the basket in line with the rim. Emphasize a full arm extension, proper rotation on the ball (backspin), and a full follow-through when finishing the shot.

Variations: Players must swish one shot before changing spots.
A second variation is for players to make as many shots in a row as possible before changing spots.
A third variation is for the players to close the eyes and make one shot before changing.

Shooting Release from the Knees

Divide the squad evenly among the available baskets. Partners alternate shooting. Three shooting spots are designated around the basket. Players take five shots from each spot while kneeling on the floor. The spots are the same as in the previous drill.

Variations: Players alternate turns shooting from each spot and attempt to make as many consecutive shots as possible.
A second variation is for the players to stay at a particular spot until one is swished.

Follow Through in Place

Squad members are divided evenly at all available baskets. Players alternate shooting from different spots around the basket. One player at each basket selects a spot within six feet of the basket, and concentrates on proper release, arm extension, and follow-through on all shooting attempts. The object is to shoot and count the number made in a row. All players in the group shoot from the same spot. The player making the greatest number in a row selects the next spot from which to shoot. No spot may be repeated. The score is kept to determine a winner.

LAYUP SHOOTING

The skill involved in shooting layups does not receive the emphasis or concentration that it should. Many times layups are missed at crucial times in a game. A layup counts the same as any other shot made from the floor and should receive the same amount of practice-time daily to perfect it.

Half-Step Drive and Recover

Divide the squad evenly into two lines at one basket. The offensive line (O) is on the right side of the foul lane with a basketball. The defensive line (X) is at the top of the key (Diagram 7-1).

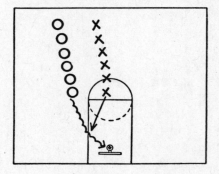

Diagram 7-1

The first players in each line face each other for a one-on-one situation. The offensive player fakes and tries to draw the defense off guard and off balance. When O feels the offensive edge, a drive is made straight to the basket using one or two dribbles for a layup. The defensive player recovers and trys to prevent the layup without fouling. Players switch lines. After several attempts from the right side of the floor, the drill is repeated on the left side.

Backboard Twisting

Players are paired off at all available baskets. Partners alternate turns shooting. On a starting signal from you, one partner at each basket shoots a variety of layups using the backboard. Each player must make five pivoting, twisting, or reverse type layups using the backboard before stopping. Players continue alternating and shooting until the time period is up. The object of the drill is to develop a feel for using the backboard from different angles while using different twisting maneuvers around the basket.

Down the Lane

The players are organized in a single line at half court with a basketball. Two players are selected as defenders (Diagram 7-2).

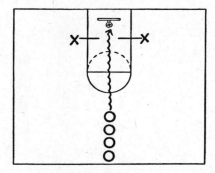

Diagram 7-2

The defenders (X) are stationed across the foul lane midway between the basket and foul line. Each defender has the outside foot in contact with the foul lane and the inside arm stretched across the lane. The offensive players (O) drive down the lane through the defense for a layup. The defensive players attempt to knock the ball loose or distract the shooter in anyway possible without fouling. After several opportunities the defensive players switch. Offensive players alternate driving with both the left and right hand. The objective is to make a layup while protecting the ball and driving through traffic.

Airborne Control

Divide the squad into two lines. Station one line at the top of the circle with a basketball. Station the other line in the left corner. The first corner player starts running along the baseline to the basket. The first passer lobs a soft pass toward the basket. The receiver jumps in the air to catch the ball and in the same motion without landing shoots a layup. Players go to the opposite line after passing and shooting.

Variations: The receiver starts in the right corner with the passer at the top of the key.

A second variation is for the receiver to start at the top of the circle and move down the lane. The passer is stationed in the left or right corner-wing area.

A third variation is for the receiver to be stationed in the low-post area with the passer in a normal wing position.

Loose Drop Pickup

Each player has a basketball in one of two lines at midcourt. Each line is facing one of the main baskets (Diagram 7-3).

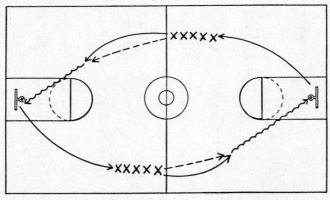

Diagram 7-3

Sound a whistle to start the drill. The first player in each line begins by rolling their basketball toward the basket they are facing. They sprint to recover the ball and shoot a right-hand layup. One dribble for control and balance is allowed. Each player recovers the basketball and moves to the end of the other line. The next players in line start rolling their basketball when the player in front of them is shooting their layup. After a three-minute period, the lines reverse direction and move in to shoot left-hand layups.

Variation: The player behind tosses the ball in front so the shooter must locate the ball before recovering it and shooting a layup.

Locate and Power Up

Players are paired off at a basket, and two balls are used. One player is responsible for placing both basketballs on the floor around the basket but inside the foul lane. The partner locates a ball and, without dribbling, jumps and lays the ball off the backboard to score. As soon as the player lands, the other ball is located and the same layup maneuver is executed. Meanwhile, the partner has rebounded the first ball and placed it in a new location on the floor. Partners alternate shooting and placing basketballs on the floor after five layups have been made.

Variations: Right-handed layups only are shot from both the left and right side of the basket after recovering the ball.

A second variation is to shoot left-handed layups only from both the left and right side of the basket after recovering the ball.

Follow a Leader

Each player has a basketball and is placed in a group of three or four at a basket. The first player in each group makes an offensive move and shoots a layup. All players in the groups "follow the leader" and execute the same maneuver. The drill continues for a specified period of time with the same player remaining as the leader.

Variations: Every layup must be preceded by a crossover dribble maneuver.

A second variation is that every layup must be preceded by a reverse or spin dribble maneuver.

A final variation is that every layup must be preceded by a stop-and-go (hesitation) maneuver.

JUMP SHOOTING

The jump shot is the most effective offensive weapon in basketball. It requires balance, coordination, and timing to execute it properly. Jump-shooting technique must be practiced daily. The following drills are designed to improve jump-shooting accuracy by exposing players to the situations and conditions that will occur in a game.

Repeat the Shot

Each player has a basketball and is placed in a group of three or four at a basket. The first player in each group is the leader. Preceding each jump shot, the shooter executes a dribble maneuver. The jump shot is taken from a distance of fifteen to eighteen feet from the basket anywhere on the perimeter. The next player in line executes the same maneuver. After all players have shot, the leader starts again shooting from a different position on the floor. The drill continues for a period of time designated by you.

Variations: The perimeter jump shot must be preceded by a crossover dribble maneuver.

A second variation is the jump shot must be preceded by a reverse or spin-dribble maneuver.

A final variation is the jump shot must be preceded by a stop-and-go maneuver.

Shot Distraction

Divide the squad into groups of three or four at a basket. One basketball is used in each group (Diagram 7-4). Player A starts with the basketball standing underneath the basket. Players B, C, and D spread themselves around the perimeter in a semicircle about fifteen feet from the basket. A passes the ball to B. After the ball is released, A charges straight toward B attempting to distract or disturb shooting concentration. B immediately sets a position upon receiving the pass, and without dribbling, takes a jump shot. B follows immediately for a rebound after shooting. A replaces B on the perimeter. B rebounds

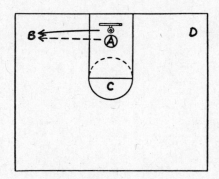

Diagram 7-4

and passes to C or D and follows to distract the shooter. Emphasis is on the receiver shooting quickly and attempting to rebound a missed shot before it hits the floor.

Around the Horn

Players pair off at a basket with one basketball. One player shoots while the partner rebounds the ball and passes it back. The ball is shot from the five basic perimeter positions around the court at a distance of fifteen to eighteen feet (right baseline corner—right wing—top of key—left wing—left baseline corner position). The shooter receives three shots from each designated spot. The rebounder retrieves the shots and passes the ball back. The rebounder concentrates on moving into position on the shots to analyze the angle of rebound and attempt to retrieve the missed shot before it hits the floor. After the shooter moves around the perimeter to each spot, players switch positions.

Variations: The rebounder retrieves missed shots before they hit the floor and makes a layup before passing the ball back out.

A second variation is the shooter must make one jump at a spot before moving to a new position on the floor.

A third variation is to record the fewest number of shots needed to make one shot from each position.

Semicircle Release

Divide the squad in half. One group is at each main basket. Three to four balls are used in each group. Two players are retrievers in the lane under the basket. The rest of the group forms a semicircle ten feet from the basket. The rebounders return eight to ten passes apiece to the perimeter shooters. After accomplishing this, they replace two other players on the perimeter who step into the lane to become rebounders. After a specified period of time designated by you, the semicircle moves back to fifteen feet.

Variations: Players make three shots on the perimeter and then replace a rebounder.

A second variation is for the players to make one shot and then move to another spot on the perimeter.

A third variation is for the players to move one dribble to the left or right after receiving a pass before taking a jump shot.

FREE THROW SHOOTING

Free throw shooting will always be a major factor in the outcome of a game. Unfortunately, many players view the practice of free throws as a rest period and consequently do not develop a consistent rhythm nor do they focus their full concentration on proper technique. When one considers the numerous games that may be won or lost on free throws, it becomes vitally important to develop the skill to the best possible degree. The following drills provide variation and supply the element of competition and pressure in improving free throw shooting percentage.

Shoot One and Rotate

All players have a basketball and start at a basket of their choice. Players shoot one free throw at their respective basket. If the attempt is successful, the player moves to the next basket on the right to shoot a free throw. Players continue around the gym moving to the right and shooting one free throw at each basket. If a free throw is missed, one lap is run to the left back to the basket where the free throw was missed. Another free throw is taken before moving on.

Variation: Players rotate one basket to the left on a successful free throw and run laps to the right on a miss.

Number in a Row

Players pair off at a basket with one basketball. One player steps to the foul line and shoots a free throw. The shooting continues until a free throw is missed. The goal is to make as many free throws in a row as possible. The partner rebounds all shooting attempts. The rule when stepping to the free throw line is to shoot until a free throw is made, and then continue shooting until one is missed.

Variation: After both players have shot, they move to another basket and continue the drill. At the conclusion of each basket, the loser is assessed some form of running. Consistant losers should be assigned extra free throw shooting at the end of practice.

Distance Progression

Players pair off at a basket with one basketball. One player rebounds. The partner stands directly in front of the rim approximately three feet away. The ball is shot in the same fashion as a free throw. After each shot, one normal step is taken backward. The shooter continues shooting and stepping back until the free throw line is reached. After taking a free throw, one step forward is taken and a shot is attempted until the player is back to the starting position. Players alternate turns shooting and rebounding.

Variations: Partners shoot one step at a time and continue shooting only while they make them.

A second variation is for the players to make two shots at each spot before moving back.

A third variation is for the players to count the number of shots necessary to make one from each spot. The lowest total wins.

Swish One

Players pair off at a basket with one basketball. One player shoots free throws while the partner rebounds. The shooter continues shooting free throws until one is "swished." Partners alternate shooting on the swish. When both players have swished a free throw they move to another basket. A record is kept and the winner is the player swishing the shot in the fewest attempts.

Blindfold Accuracy

Players pair off at a basket with one basketball. One player rebounds while the partner shoots free throws. The shooter, after establishing a position, closes the eyes when releasing the shot. Each player must make one free throw with the eyes closed before moving off the free throw line. When both partners have made one free throw, they move to another basket. A record is kept and the winner is the player making a free throw in the fewest attempts.

One and One Choose

Players pair off at a basket with a basketball. Each partner alternates shooting a one and one at the free throw line. If the first shot is made, the player attempts a second free throw. Periodically, you call out a player's name. When this happens, the designated player shoots a free throw representing the team. If it is made, the drill continues as normal with partners alternating shooting turns. If the shot is missed, all players are assigned to run.

Up and Down

Players pair off at a basket with a basketball. One player rebounds while the partner shoots free throws. The drill starts at three free throw attempts. The shooter must make all three. If successful, two shots in a row must be made the next time. If successful again, the next time one free throw must be made. If a player fails to convert the designated number of free throws in a row, the next time at the free throw line the total to make increases by one. Example: Make three in a row—miss—make four in a row—make three in a row—make two in a row—make one. Usually this drill is run at the end of practice because of the potential time factor involved. Partners making their free throws are excused with the remaining players paired off with someone else.

"Official" Drill

Players divide into groups of three at a basket. One basketball is used in each group. One player rebounds the free throw attempts. One player is at the free throw line shooting. The third player is the "official." The "official" hands the ball to the shooter for a free throw. After five free throws, players rotate positions. On a miss, the rebounder attempts to tap the ball in before returning the ball to the free throw line.

HOOK SHOOTING

The hook shot is often neglected in practice but is definitely an offensive weapon with great potential, especially in the low-post area. This becomes particularly true when the offensive low post is outsized by the defender and unable to power the ball into the basket. Also, most players either by design or by situation will end up at one time or another in the lane or low post. Consequently, it is necessary to be familiar with the hook shot as a potential offensive threat.

Continuous Release

Players pair off at a basket with one basketball and alternate turns shooting. One partner starts with a basketball in front of the basket. The player starts the drill by stepping to the right side of the basket with the left foot and shoots a short right-hand hook shot off the backboard. The player grabs the ball as it comes through the net without letting it touch the floor, then takes a pivot on the left foot without dribbling. The player continues movement by stepping to the left side of the basket with the right foot and shoots a short left-hand hook shot off the backboard. After rebounding the ball, a pivot is taken on the right foot and a step across with the left foot to shoot a short right-hand hook shot off the backboard. This back and forth continuous hook shooting action continues until the player has made ten shots.

Variation: Players execute the same drill but as they are releasing the ball they close their eyes to develop a "feel" for using the backboard.

Free Throw Lane to Middle

Players divide into groups of three at a basket. Two basketballs are used (Diagram 7-5). B and C have a basketball. A starts in a low-lane position even with the basket and facing B. Both feet are flat on

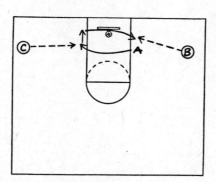

Diagram 7-5

the floor. B passes to A. A drop-steps into the lane with the right foot and shoots a left-hand hook shot. After shooting, A moves across the lane and establishes a low-lane position on the other side. B rebounds the shot and returns to the wing position. C passes into A when the new position is established. A drop-steps into the lane with the left foot and shoots a right-hand hook shot. C follows for the rebound. A continues back and forth across the lane to receive passes from B and C for hook shots. After A has taken three hook shots each way, players rotate positions.

Variations: Upon receiving a pass, the shooter drop-steps toward the baseline to take a hook shot.

A second variation is for the shooter to take one dribble across the lane for a hook shoot after receiving the ball.

Lane to Baseline Move

Players are divided into groups of three at a basket. One basketball is used in each group (Diagram 7-6). A is the shooter and stands outside the lane in a position even with the bottom of the free throw circle. B has a basketball in the corner. C is standing in the lane to rebound. B passes to A. A slide-steps down the lane with the left foot leading. When the line of the basket is reached, a pivot is taken on the left foot and a right-handed hook shot is attempted. A returns to position after the shot. C rebounds the shot and passes to B in the corner. A is ready to receive another pass. After five shots, players rotate positions. When all have had a turn, the players move to the other side of the floor.

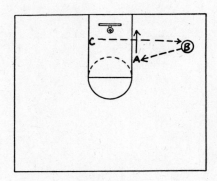

Diagram 7-6

Lane Drive Hook Shot

Players divide into groups of three at a basket. Two basketballs are used in each group (Diagram 7-7). A is the shooter and starts in a low-post position. B and C have a basketball in a wing position. B starts the drill by passing to A. A turns into the lane pivoting on the right foot and drives across for a left-hand hook shot off the backboard. B follows for the rebound and returns to the original position. A sets up in the low post on the left side. C passes to A. A turns back into the lane pivoting on the left foot and drives across for a right-hand hook shot off the backboard. C rebounds the shot and returns to the wing position. The drill continues until A has shot three left- and right-hand hook shots driving across the lane. Players then rotate positions.

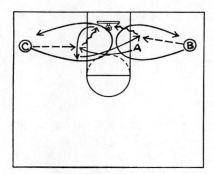

Diagram 7-7

Lane to Lane Hook

Players divide into groups of three at a basket. Two basketballs are used in each group (Diagram 7-7). A lines up outside the lane even with the bottom of the free throw circle. B and C have a basketball and line up even with the top of the circle about five feet outside the lane. B starts the drill by passing to A. A dribbles into the lane for a hook shot and then moves across the lane to set up on the other side. B follows down the middle to rebound the shot and circles back out to the base position. On the other side, C passes in to A. A drives into the lane for a hook shot and continues across to the other side. C follows for a rebound and circles back out with the ball. A receives three passes from each side for hook shots. Players rotate.

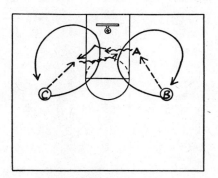

Diagram 7-8

Match the Leader

Players divide into groups of three at a basket. Each player has a basketball. One player in the group acts as the "leader" and proceeds to shoot any kind of hook shot inside the lane. The other two players must follow and execute the same hook shot and maneuver. Each player is the "leader" for five hook shots.

Variations: A game of "horse" is played. A letter is assigned for each missed shot.

A second variation is to play a game of "match." Plus one is scored for each hook shot made. Minus one is scored for each hook shot missed. The game goes to eleven points with the losers assigned some type of penalty.

BACKBOARD SHOOTING

Using the backboard in shooting is an important skill to be learned on different playing courts. The tension or tightness of rims will vary; but if a basketball is placed properly off the backboard, the rebound angle will remain consistent. Particularly on close shots, the backboard will make the difference between scoring and missing in many cases. Developing backboard shooting skill and confidence is time well spent.

Consecutive Bank Shots

Players pair off at a basket with one basketball. The shooter stands on the foul lane at an angle of 45 degrees from the backboard, attempting to make consecutive shots off the backboard while the partner rebounds. Partners alternate turns and sides of the basket. In the second round, players shoot from a distance of nine feet. The third round is from twelve feet. The fourth round is from fifteen feet.

Pivot-Square-Bank-Recover

Players pair off at a basket with one basketball. One player starts with the basketball outside the lane on either side of the basket and shoots a jump shot off the backboard. After the shot, a move is made across the lane to the other side of the basket. The partner rebounds the shot and passes the ball back. Each time the ball is received, the shooter must pivot and square to the basket for a jump shot off the backboard before moving back across the lane. Three jump shots are taken from both sides of the basket before players switch.

Variations: The shooter pivots toward the base line to square off for a jump shot.

A second variation is for the shooter to pivot toward the middle to square off for a jump shot.

Percentage Score

Players pair off at a basket with one basketball. One player is the shooter. The partner is the rebounder. The shooter takes jump shots from the left side of the basket from ten to twelve feet away. All shots must be off the backboard. Designate the percentage goal out of groups of ten shots. The shooter must make the percentage before switching with the partner. Example: 70 percent is making seven to ten shots attempted. After both players have attained the percentage from the left side, they switch to the right side of the basket. The percentage goal is increased as backboard shooting ability improves.

SPOT SHOOTING

The ability to shoot quickly and accurately from specific areas on the floor is especially important against zone defense. Often a shooting opportunity is presented only for a split second. Players must develop the skill to recognize the opening, quickly release the shot in balance, and possess the confidence that the shot will be made. The following drills will aid players to shoot confidently from different areas on the floor.

Sink One

Players pair off at a basket with one basketball. Various spots on the floor are designated by you. Players alternate turns shooting from the spots. The spots are set up in groups of three and players shoot from a specific spot until they make one. Competition can be arranged with partners matching each other from the various spots by keeping a record of the least number of shots needed to make one.

Make-Miss

Players pair off at a basket with one basketball. Various spots are designated on the floor by you. One player shoots jump shots while the partner rebounds. The shooter makes as many shots in a row as possible, and then continues shooting until missing. Partners alternate shooting and rebounding from all spots.

Drop Three

Players pair off at a basket with one basketball. One player shoots and the partner rebounds. The shooter moves to a spot on the floor designated by you and shoots jump shots until making three. Players then switch. Each time they shoot, they move to a new spot on the floor. A game can be played by having players compete against each other. The fewest number of shots necessary to make three is the winner.

Free Throw Lane Spots

Players pair off at a basket with one basketball. Seven specific spots are designated to shoot from (Diagram 7-9).

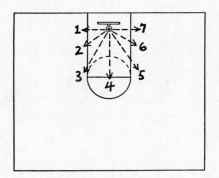

Diagram 7-9

The spots are:

1. Outside of the lane even with the basket on the left side.
2. Halfway between the basket and free throw line on the left side of the basket in the midlane position.
3. Juncture of the foul lane and free throw line on the left side of the basket.

4. Middle of the free throw line.
5. Juncture of the foul lane and free throw line on the right side of the basket.
6. Halfway between the basket and free throw line on the right side of the basket in the midlane position.
7. Outside of the lane even with the basket on the right side.

Partners alternate turns shooting and rebounding as they move around the inside lane spots. Several varied methods of improving shooting proficiency from the different spots are used.

1. Partners shoot one from each spot and record the number of made and missed shots.
2. Partners stay at each spot until one shot is made. The total number of shots to accomplish this is recorded.
3. Partners alternate turns shooting from each spot. They shoot until they make one and continue until they miss one. The number of shots made in a row is recorded.

Variations: The first time around the spots the players start with the ball while facing the basket. A second variation is to have the players start with their back to the basket. They must pivot to the basket before shooting.

Outside Perimeter Spots

Players pair off at a basket with one basketball. Seven outside perimeter spots are designated eighteen feet from the basket (Diagram 7-10).

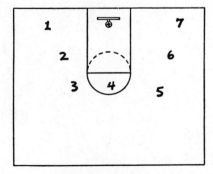

Diagram 7-10

The spots are:

1. Even with the basket on the left baseline in the corner.
2. Midway between the basket and the free throw line on the left side.
3. One step inside the top of the circle and outside the free throw circle on the left side.
4. Midway between the free throw line and top of the circle in line with the basket.
5. One step inside the top of the circle and outside the free throw circle on the right side.
6. Midway between the basket and the free throw line on the right side.
7. Even with the basket on the left baseline in the corner.

Partners alternate shooting and rebounding as they move around the outside perimeter spots. The same shooting methods employed in the previous drill are used to improve skill, concentration, and develop the spirit of competition.

8
Improving jumping ability and offensive rebounding techniques

In order to score, a team must have the basketball. The best means for getting possession of the ball is by rebounding. The team that controls the backboards will control the outcome of the game.

Rebounding is divided into offensive and defensive phases. Both phases must be developed and practiced to provide ball possession at both ends of the floor. The important attributes in becoming an effective rebounder are balance, timing, jumping ability, and anticipation.

Practice sessions must be designed to incorporate rebounding sense. This is accomplished with drills including both one-on-one situations and team-oriented concepts. Isolating techniques will teach all players the proper mechanics of offensive rebounding skills. In addition, drills must include physical contact which, by nature, is inherent in rebounding. Observing and learning the angles of rebound for shots from various positions on the floor will aid in the rebounding development.

MUSCLE READINESS

Stretching and loosening up the various muscle groups is necessary before engaging in any type of jumping movement. Proper preparation prevents muscle soreness and/or disability. Muscle response may be improved by properly and sufficiently warming up.

Loose Run and Bounce

Players spread out in random formation around the court. On your signal, the players start running "loose" in place. A good description of this movement pattern would be shadow boxing. The feet land lightly with the arms and shoulders loosely manipulated. The legs are moved up and down, forward and back, side to side, and also in a front-to-back scissors fashion. Run the drill for fifteen seconds.

Variations: The loose running form is done while holding a basketball in various positions for control.

A second variation is to perform the loose running form with the eyes closed. This allows for feeling the different foot pressures necessary to maintain balance and control.

Side and Back

Players spread out in random formation around the court. On your signal, the players move feet apart to the side (shoulder width) and back together. The continuous opening and closing of the legs is done as quickly as possible for a ten-second time interval.

Variations: The players hold a basketball in front of the body, overhead, and behind the back while executing the drill.

A second variation is to have the players close their eyes while executing the same maneuvers.

Forward and Back

The players are spread out in random formation around the court. Each player stands erect with one foot in advance of the other. The heel of the lead foot is in line with the toe of the trail foot. A rapid shifting of the feet forward and backward is accomplished by moving the legs from the hips. Concentration is always on the heel of the lead foot being in line with the toe of the trail foot when switching. Ten second time intervals are recommended for the quick transition.

Variations: The players hold a basketball in various positions while performing the drill. A second variation is to have the players close their eyes while executing the drill.

Hopscotch

Players spread out in random formation. On your command, players perform the following jumping maneuvers: jump off left foot, land on right foot, jump off right foot, land on both feet, jump off both feet, and land on left foot to complete one circuit. Three consecutive circuits are done before the sequence is reversed starting with a right-foot hop.

Variation: Players line up on the end line. On your signal, players execute jumping sequence by moving forward to cover a length of the court and back again.

Hop on Down

Players spread out in random formation and start jumping together on command from you. They proceed to jump off both feet three times forward. This is immediatley followed by three hops back, three hops left, and three hops right. When finished, they repeat the sequence by hopping twice in all directions and then by hopping once in each direction before stopping.

JUMPING READINESS

The art of jumping is a vital skill in basketball. It is a major ingredient for rebounding, tapping, shooting, blocking shots, deflecting passes, and winning jump balls. Jumping ability varies among individuals because of heredity, body type, and musculature. However, practice will improve timing and help develop jumping ability to a greater degree.

On Command-Release

Players spread out in random formation around the court. Each time a whistle is sounded by you, the players respond by jumping and extending one arm upward as in a center jump situation. Each jumping maneuver is preceded by a short (four to six inches) preparatory step followed by a similar closing of the trail foot before exploding upward.

Variations: On the whistle, the players jump with both arms extended as in rebounding a shot.

A second variation involves a basketball. The players toss their ball in the air and time their jump to recover it at the highest possible point.

A third variation is to have the players bounce their ball off the floor in front of them and continue to recover it at the highest possible point.

A final variation is to have the players close their eyes and jump with a left arm extension, right arm extension and both arm extension in the rebounding position.

Consecutive Spot Touching

Players spread out around the court facing a backboard or wall. On your command, the players jump and touch a spot (rim—backboard—spot on wall). Immediately upon landing, the players regather and jump again to touch the same spot. This procedure continues for a ten-second interval. The time of intervals is lengthened in succeeding practice sessions as the legs become stronger.

Variations: The consecutive spot touching is done with the nondominant hand.

A second variation is to spot-touch with both hands simultaneously.

A third variation is to spot-touch by alternating hands on each touch.

A final variation is to touch the spot continuously while holding a basketball.

Squad Matchups

Players split into groups of three by size and/or jumping ability. Each group has a basketball. Two players in each group line up in a jump ball circle. The third player is the "official" and tosses the ball. The two jumpers attempt to control the tap. After either jumper taps the ball, both jumpers attempt to recover the ball. However, the ball must touch the floor first before either player recovers it. The player recovering the ball tosses it in the next center jump.

One-on-One with a Ball Toss

Players split into groups of three by size and/or ability. Each group has a basketball. Two players in each group line up in a center jump circle. The third player tosses the ball. Both jumpers attempt to gain possession of the ball after the tap. The ball must hit the floor first. Whichever player recovers the ball is on offense. The other jumper plays defense. A game of one-on-one is played for one basket or one missed shot. If the shot is made, the scorer tosses the next jump ball. If a shot is missed and rebounded by the defender, this person tosses the ball for the next jump.

Step-Gather-Release

Players line up on the end line. They start together on your signal. They step forward with the left foot, close right foot and jump straight up off both feet. The same sequence is continued for a full length. Upon returning, players step first with the right and close with the left foot before jumping.

Variations: Players slide right foot laterally and close with the left to initiate a jump. This continues for a length before returning and sliding with the left foot laterally first. Players step back with the right foot and close with the left foot before jumping. The same procedure as before is followed.

AGGRESSIVENESS

Because of the fast-paced nature of basketball, most phases will involve some degree of physical contact. The officials enforcing the basketball rules will keep the amount of contact allowed under control. However, there are numerous situations in which contact cannot be minimized or eliminated. The players must realize that contact is part of the game and must be exposed to the possibility of contact through structured drills.

Anything Will Happen

Place the players in groups of three or four by size. One basketball is used in each group. Impose a thirty-second time limit.

All players in the group stand inside the free throw lane and face the basket. You or a manager starts play with a basketball at the free throw line. The ball is shot at the basket to start the drill. All players attempt to rebound the basketball and score. Play is continuous as players keep rebounding made or missed shots and attempt to score a basket for themselves. The player with the most baskets within the thirty-second time limit is the winner. All players must stay inside the lane and only one dribble is allowed before shooting.

Variations: The player scoring the most baskets is allowed to rest in the next thirty-second session.

A second variation is to run a single elimination contest with the winner of each thirty-second match stepping outside the lane. Competition continues until one player is left.

Butt to Butt

All players pair off in random formation around the court. Size and ability should be taken into consideration for the pairings. Partners stand back to back. Their knees are flexed to lower the center of gravity. On a signal from you, both players attempt to bump each other forward by butting buttocks. The first player forced to move one or both feet forward to keep balance is the loser.

Variation: Both partners dribble a basketball while attempting to knock each other off balance.

Secure a Rebound

Place the entire team around a basket inside the free throw lane. A rebounding or shooting rim is attached to the basket. You or a manager shoots from various spots around the perimeter from fifteen to eighteen feet away. When a player gets a rebound, a step is taken outside of the lane. The single elimination continues until there is only one player left who has not gotten a rebound.

Variations: Split the players into two groups of forwards and guards to equalize rebounding opportunity.

A second variation is to allow the player securing a rebound a chance to watch the rest of the team run a sprint.

A third variation is to have the last layer left without a rebound run a sprint.

TAPPING

The ability to tap a basketball under control is important to increase scoring possibilities and to keep the ball "alive" on the backboard. Often a rebound or score occurs on the third, fourth, or fifth tap on a play.

Continuous Tapping

Each player has a basketball and is assigned to a basket. On your signal, all players begin jumping and tapping the ball with both hands simultaneously. The ball is continuously tapped under control for twenty seconds. The ball is positioned off to the side of the rim on the backboard even with the height of the rim. Three sets tapping for twenty seconds with a ten-second rest interval between sets are done.

Variations: The basketball is tapped for three twenty-second sets with the right hand only.

A second variation is to tap the ball with the left hand only.

A final variation is to tap the ball alternating left and right hands on each tap.

Partners' Tapping

Players pair off at a basket with a basketball. Partners stand on opposite sides of the basket facing the backboard. On your signal, all groups start together. One player tosses the ball over the rim off the backboard to a partner. The partner taps the ball back to the other side off the backboard using both hands. Partners continue tapping their basketball back and forth over the rim for thirty seconds.

Variations: Partners tap the ball back and forth continuously using the right hand only for thirty seconds.

A second variation is to tap the ball back and forth using the left hand only.

Three and In

Players pair off at a basket with one basketball. Partners alternate turns with one partner working at a time. One player stands to the side of the rim and tosses the ball off the backboard. The ball is tapped three times off the backboard and then the fourth one is tapped in.

Variations: The ball is tapped with both hands on the right side of the basket.

A second variation is to tap the ball with both hands on the left side of the basket.

A third variation is to tap with the right hand only on the right side of the basket.

A fourth variation is to tap with the right hand on the left side of the basket.

A fifth variation is to tap the ball with the left hand on the left side of the basket.

A sixth variation is to tap the ball with the left hand on the right side of the basket.

Accuracy Tapping

Players pair off at a basket with one basketball. One player tosses the ball over the basket off the backboard to a partner. The partner times the jump to tap the ball in the basket. The ball is then tossed back over the rim off the backboard so the other partner can tap in the ball.

Variations: The ball is tapped in with two hands simultaneously.

A second variation is to tap the ball in with the right hand from the right side.

A third variation is to tap the ball in with the left hand from the left side.

A fourth variation is to alternate hands tapping the ball in on each succeeding toss.

OFFENSIVE REBOUNDING

Offensive rebounding is extremely important to offensive scoring potential. To be effective offensively, a team must be able to get second and third opportunities on missed shots. The key areas to concentrate on are recognizing the angle of rebound, quick acceleration, and lateral mobility to get to the ball.

Jump, Recover, and Score

Players pair off at a basket. One basketball is used as partners alternate turns. Each player stands with a basketball to the right side of the basket inside the lane. The ball is bounced off the floor hard enough to rebound higher than the player's reach. A jump is then timed so the ball is recovered at the peak of the jump. Upon landing, the player immediately explodes up to the basket and makes a layup off the backboard. After executing the same maneuver three times, the partner repeats the same. After both have completed the drill, they move to the left side and execute the same drill. Finally, they step in front of the basket and repeat. However, the ball is now laid over the front of the rim on the layup attempt. Players continue alternating turns at each spot.

Up-Down-Up Release

Players pair off at a basket with one basketball. Partners alternate turns from the left side of the basket for one minute and then move over to the right side. One partner tosses the ball off the backboard. A jump is timed to recover the ball at the peak off the jump. Upon landing, the player immediately explodes back up to the basket and makes a layup off the backboard.

Variations: Each player has a ball. They alternate attempts.

A second variation is for one player to throw the ball over the rim off the backboard to a partner who jumps, recovers the ball, and explodes back for a layup. After the shot, the ball is thrown over the rim back to the partner to execute the same technique.

Double Team and Up

Players divide into groups of three. A stands under the backboard facing the free throw line. B stands in front of A facing the backboard. C stands behind B with a basketball and faces the backboard (Diagram 8-1). C tosses the ball off the backboard over B's head. B jumps and rebounds the ball. As B lands, A and C attempt to prevent B from jumping back through traffic to score. Players rotate from A to B to C after each play.

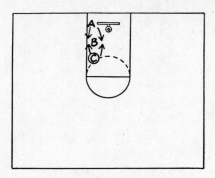

Diagram 8-1

Variations: A and C must remain on the floor at all times in attempting to prevent B from scoring.

A second variation is to allow A and C to leave the floor in attempting to prevent B from scoring.

Long Rebound Recovery

The entire squad lines up single file at the free throw line. A shooting rim or rebounding rim is attached to the basket. You have a basketball and move to different spots on the perimeter (Diagram 8-2). Shoot from different spots on the floor outside the free throw line. Each player in order waits until the ball hits the rim. An attempt is made to catch the ball before it hits the floor, but players accelerate only after the ball touches the rim. After recovery, the players go to the end of the line. The next player does not move forward, but accelerates from a spot to recover the ball. Eventually the line moves further back from the basket and it becomes increasingly difficult for the players to get to the ball before it hits the floor.

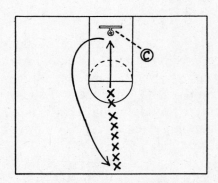

Diagram 8-2

Variations: Spread pylons out on the floor between the players and the basket. Players must negotiate the pylons to recover the ball.

A second variation is to use other obstacles such as chairs and balls to increase the difficulty in recovering the ball.

Release and Follow

The squad lines up along the side line. A shooting rim or rebounding rim is attached. Each player in turn stands on the free throw line with the back to the basket. You or a manager is positioned in front of the player with a basketball. A shot is taken. The player watches the flight of the ball. As soon as it passes out of visual range, a quick turn is made to locate the ball and rebound it before it hits the floor. Players alternate turning left and right when moving in for the rebound.

Variations: Players do not turn for the rebound until they hear the ball hit the rim.

A second variation is to add pylons after proficiency has been establishd. This increases the difficulty of getting to the basketball before it hits the floor.

Rebound Elimination

The squad divides into two or three groups by size and/or position. One group at a time steps inside the free throw lane facing the basket. You have a basketball outside the free throw line. Take a shot anywhere outside the free throw line. All players inside the lane rebound. The player rebounding steps outside the lane and passes the ball back to you. Continue shooting until there is only one player left. The loser in the single elimination rebound contest is assigned a sprint.

Variation: The entire squad is placed inside the free throw lane. You begin shooting. After each shot, the rebounder steps out of the lane. The final two players left in the lane run.

Rebound and Clear

The squad divides into groups of three. Assign each group to a basket. One basketball is used in each group. A stands underneath the backboard with the back to the end line. B stands in front of A and facing the backboard. C stands behind A with the basketball facing the backboard. C tosses the ball off the backboard over B's head. B times a jump and rebound the ball. As soon as B lands, an attempt is made to clear the ball to the corner by dribbling. At the same time A and C double-team B and attempt to prevent the ball from being cleared. Players rotate from A to B to C. After three opportunities apiece rebounding on the right side of the basket, the players switch to the left side.

Move Through Traffic

The players divide into groups of three. Player A stands underneath the backboard facing the free throw line. B stands in front of A facing the backboard in rebounding position. Player C stands behind B with a basketball. A manager is stationed in the corner. Player C throws the ball off the backboard. B jumps to rebound the ball. Upon landing, an attempt is made to pass the ball out of traffic to the corner. As B is landing with the ball, A and C attempt to prevent the ball from being passed by either deflecting it or attempting to knock it loose. After three opportunities, players rotate positions. The drill is then run from the right side of the basket and passed to the right corner.

Variation: The manager is stationed in the wing area to receive the outlet pass.

SECOND EFFORT SCORING

Developing the ability to sustain a second effort on missed shots is a vital part of a team's offensive thrust. In many cases the first shot taken by a team is missed. Consequently, the ability to rebound and get second and third opportunities to score on the same possession is extremely important.

One-on-One with a Shooter

The players divide into groups of three. One player has the ball and is designated as the shooter. The other two players are stationed in the lane. The shooter begins moving around the perimeter from fifteen to eighteen feet and takes jump shots. The two rebounders jockey for rebounding position inside the lane. The shooter continues shooting until successful. On a missed shot, the two lane players fight for the rebound and immediately attempt to score. The scorer then becomes the shooter while the original shooter steps into the lane to become a rebounder.

TEAM COMPETITION

In order to reproduce actual game situations, it is necessary to structure team competition with goals and objectives. Important aspects include shots from different floor positions to watch flight patterns and analyze angles of rebound, developing a sense of when to release the ball, establishing paths to the basket, and working on maneuvers to get open.

Two-on-Two

Players divide into two lines at the left and right wing positions, fifteen feet from the basket. The first player in each line turns and faces the next player. You stand with a basketball at the top of the key, and shoot the ball after positions are set. The object is for the second player in each line to get the ball regardless of whether the shot goes in. If the defensive player gets the ball, they move to the end of the line. The offensive players then move to defense. If the offensive players get a rebound, they move to the end of the line and the defensive players remain on defense for another series.

Three-on-Three

Players divide into three lines at the left base line, right base line, and foul line positions. The first player in each line turns to play defense on the next player in line. You stand at one wing position with a ball and a manager stands at the other wing position with a ball. On a signal either one shoots. The three offensive rebounders move after the ball. If an offensive rebound is secured, they move to the end of the line and the defensive players remain on defense for the next group. If the defensive players get the rebound, they move to the end of the line and the offensive players turn and move on defense.

Four-on-Four

Players divide into four lines at the offensive guard and forward positions. You stand at the foul line with a basketball and two managers have a basketball at either wing position. The first player in each line turns and plays defense on the next player in line. On a signal, one of the three shooters takes a shot. The offensive and defensive players converge on the rebound. If the defenders rebound, they move to the end of their respective lines and the offensive rebounders become the defensive players for the next series. If the offensive players rebound the shot, they move to the end of the line and the defensive players remain on defense for the next series.

Five-on-Five

Players divide into units of five. One group is assigned offense and one group defense. Each offensive player has a ball. You stand out-of-bounds under the basket and indicate which offensive player will shoot. The other four drop their ball and all five converge for the rebound. Teams remain on offense and defense respectively for five shots. For every offensive rebound gained, the defense is assigned a penalty sprint when the series is completed. The units alternate offense and defense after their series is completed. A variety of offensive formations are set up for rebound concentration including a one-three-one, three-two, two-one-two, two-three, and one-four.

9
Developing individual offensive techniques with the ball

Individual maneuvers with the ball are paramount in developing offensive proficiency and scoring potential. The nature of basketball dictates all players must work on the necessary skills that will enable them to escape from the defensive skills of their opponents.

Offensive moves with the ball require quickness, balance, and coordination to become an effective scorer. Penetration via the dribble is an essential offensive tool. Developing the ability to score in the three post areas (low-mid-high) are necessary in becoming a complete offensive player.

FAKES-FEINTS

Learning how to fake and feint with the ball is a prerequisite to becoming a potential scorer. These maneuvers include the jab step, crossover step, and the rocker step to set the defense up for a jump shot or a drive.

Mass Technique

Players spread out in random formation with a basketball. The players face you in a position ready to react. On your signal, the players react together and execute the specific maneuver outlined. Each specific fake is practiced with both the left and right foot as the pivot foot.

1. Jab step fake and reset foot position while moving the ball into a jump shooting position.
2. Jab step fake and go by extending one step and taking one dribble in the driving direction.
3. Rocker step fake and slide foot back to reset while moving the ball into a jump shooting position.
4. Rocker step fake—slide back and go extending one step and taking one dribble in the driving direction.
5. Crossover step fake and reset while moving the ball into jump shooting position.
6. Crossover step fake and go by extending one step and taking one dribble in the driving direction.

Line Shooting

Players pair off at a basket. Every player has a basketball and faces a basket fifteen feet away. All maneuvers outlined in the previous drill are executed on command from you. Each time a maneuver is completed, the players execute a jump shot or drive to the basket for a layup to finish the play. When the players recover their basketball, they move to a new position on the floor and wait for the next command.

Variations: Designate the specific maneuver to be executed on a signal.

The second variation is for you to designate the specific area on the floor where the particular maneuver will be executed.

Token Defense

Divide the squad into groups of four at a basket. Players work in pairs and alternate playing offense and defense. Designate which faking maneuver to execute. The offensive player has a basketball and faces the basket from fifteen feet away. The defensive player assumes a balanced guarding stance at a normal distance (arms length away) from the offensive player. However, the hands are held behind the back and remain there throughout the maneuver. On a whistle, the offensive player executes the designated fake and either resets for the jump shot or drives to the basket for a layup. The defense moves with the offense but cannot use the hands throughout the maneuver.

Full Go Defense

Divide the squad into groups of three at a basket. The offensive player is A, defensive player is B, and C is the passer (Diagram 9-1). C passes to A. B moves into a guarding position on A. A executes a faking maneuver and plays one-on-one against B until A scores or B rebounds a missed shot. Players rotate from offense to defense to passer. The offensive maneuvers will be performed from the top of the key, the corners, and the wing positions.

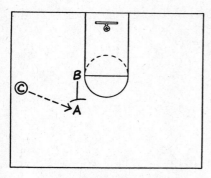

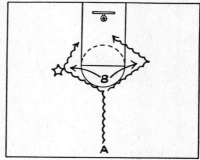

Diagram 9-1   *Diagram 9-2*

Dribble Fake Drive

Divide the squad in half. Line A stands at half court with a basketball. Line B is stationed on the side line (Diagram 9-2). B stands at the top of the free throw circle in a defensive stance position. A starts dribbling straight down the middle toward the basket. As A approaches B, an attempt is made to set B up and drive to the basket. B meanwhile is establishing a good defensive position to stop A. A may execute a reverse (spin) dribble maneuver, crossover dribble maneuver, or a hesitation (stutter) maneuver to score. Players switch lines at the conclusion of play.

Variations: The offensive player drives from the base line corner position. The defense attacks from the lane.
     A second variation is for the offensive player to drive from the wing position. The defense attacks from the juncture of the free throw line and foul lane.

PIVOTING

Pivoting is a basketball fundamental specifically used to protect the basketball from defensive pressure. It is extremely important in rebounding, dribbling, driving, and keeping possession of the ball after dribbling has stopped and a pass cannot be made.

Mass Pivoting Technique

Players spread out in random formation facing you. All pivoting maneuvers involve turns of 180 degrees or halfway around to face the opposite way. The players are instructed in the mechanics of both the forward and reverse pivots. The teaching sequence is:

1. Execute a forward pivot on the left foot on each blast of the whistle.
2. Execute a forward pivot on the right foot on each blast of the whistle.
3. Execute a reverse pivot on the left foot on each blast of the whistle.
4. Execute a forward pivot on the right foot on each blast of the whistle.
5. Indicate which foot to pivot on by first pointing with the corresponding hand, and immediately call out the type of pivot to be executed.

On all pivots the players respond as quickly as possible and assume ready position for the next command.

Variations: Each player starts with the back to you and listens for your signal. Call out quickly the foot to pivot on and the type of pivot to execute in rapid order.

A second variation is for each player to have a ball and execute the designated techniques while positioning the ball as if protecting it from a defensive opponent.

A third variation is for the players to perform all pivoting maneuvers with their eyes closed. It is important to develop an awareness and feel of the change of body position while maintaining balance.

Pivot and Slide

Organize the players in groups of three on the end line. Each group has a basketball. The first player stands sideways with the right shoulder pointing downcourt. On a signal from you, the players slide to the right two steps while dribbling. After the two steps, a reverse pivot is executed on the right foot. Each player continues sliding and dribbling two steps to the left and then reverse pivots on the left foot. The sliding, dribbling, and reverse pivoting is done the full length of the court and back. When the first player returns, the next player in the group goes.

Ball Toss—Pivot and Pass

Organize the players in groups of three on the end line. Each group has a basketball. The first player in each group begins by tossing the ball eight to ten feet out in front so that it bounces on the floor. The player sprints and recovers the ball with a two-foot jump stop. After recovering the ball, a pivot is done so the player faces the next person in line and the ball is passed back. The pass is followed to the end of the line. The drill is continuous with each player in line tossing the ball, recovering it, executing a pivot, and passing back.

Variations: Players execute a forward pivot on the left foot.
A second variation is for players to execute a forward pivot on the right foot.
A third variation is for players to execute reverse pivots on the left and right foot.

OFFENSIVE MANEUVERS
FROM THE LOW POST

The low post is that area located around the basket which includes the first lane space on either side. All players should become familiar with the offensive moves around this area. It is not uncommon for most players to find themselves at one time or another positioned in the low post. Therefore, all players should have an adequate knowledge of how to be a scoring threat in the low post.

Turn and Score

Players pair off at a basket with a basketball. One player stands on the block (first lane space) with the back to the basket. The partner with the ball stands twenty feet from the basket in the corner. The ball is passed into the low-post player. The post receives the ball with both feet stationary. After receiving the ball, the receiver immediately pivots to face the basket and jumps off both feet for a power layup.

No dribbling is allowed. Each partner receives three shots before switching positions. The four pivoting maneuvers are executed from the right low-post position before switching to the left low-post position.

1. Drop step with the right foot for a banked layup.
2. Drop step with the left foot for a banked layup.
3. Forward pivot on the right foot for a banked layup.
4. Forward pivot on the left foot for a banked layup.

Outside Pivot Foot Turn

The players pair off at a basket with a basketball. One player stands in the left low-post position. The partner is in the corner twenty feet from the basket with a basketball. The ball is passed high into the low post. The post designates the left foot as the pivot foot (closest to the basket). At the same time a step is taken toward the incoming pass with the right foot and the right hand is extended as a target. This technique lengthens the receiving area. Upon reception, the player pivots on the left foot toward the baseline and takes a jump shot upon facing the basket. Three passes are received for the pivot and jump shot before switching with the partner. After both players have executed, they switch to the right side of the floor. The receiver then steps forward with the left foot and extends the left hand as a target area. The pivot is done on the right foot toward the baseline for the jump shot.

Inside Pivot Foot Turn

The players pair off at a basket with a basketball. One player stands in the left low-position. The partner is twenty feet away in the wing area (free throw line extended) with a basketball. The receiver uses the inside foot (right) as the pivot foot. The left hand is extended as a target while stepping out with the left foot to meet the pass. After reception, the player pivots on the right foot into the lane and shoots a jump shot. No dribbling is allowed. After three shots, the partner executes the drill. Players then switch sides and operate from the right low-post position. The receiver uses the left foot as the pivot foot. The right hand is extended and a step taken forward with the right foot to receive the pass. The player then pivots on the left foot into the lane for a jump shot.

Token Defense

The players divide into groups of three at a basket with one basketball. A is the passer from the wing area. B is the receiver in the low post. C is the defender (Diagram 9-3). Each player receives three shots from the low-post area. Players then rotate from passer to defense to offense. The following series of defensive techniques are used to develop low post offensive skills:

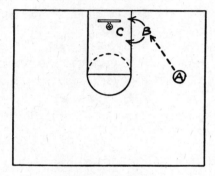

Diagram 9-3

1. The defender allows the ball to be received by the low post. After reception, the defender contests the offensive maneuver but may not leave the floor at any time.
2. The defender allows the ball to be received by the low post. After reception, the defender contests the offensive maneuver and may leave the floor to do so.
3. The defender contests the pass into the low post. If the pass is completed, the defender continues playing defense but may not leave the floor.
4. The defender plays full go.

OFFENSIVE MANEUVERS IN THE MIDPOST

The midpost position is located on either side of the free throw lane even with the bottom of the free throw circle. Many times offensive opportunities are presented in the midpost area as defensive adjustments for coverage must be made. All players should be acquainted with the midpost area to take advantage of opportunities when they develop.

Pivot to Middle for Jumper

The players divide into groups of three at a basket with one ball. Player A lines up in the left midpost position with the back to the basket. B lines up in the wing position on the same side as the midpost. C is under the basket to rebound the ball and return it to B (Diagram 9-4). Player A receives the ball by stepping to meet the pass with the right foot while extending the right hand as a target. Upon reception A pivots on the left foot and steps into the lane facing the basket for a jump shot. C passes back to B; A receives five passes and makes the same pivot for a jump shot. Players then switch from A to B to C. After all have had their turn, play is switched to the other side of the floor. The pivot is now on the right foot into the lane for a jumper after squaring to the basket.

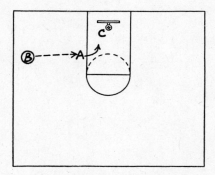

Diagram 9-4

Pivot and Drive the Middle

Players divide into groups of three at a basket. The same player position is used as in the previous drill. When the pass is made, the midpost receives the ball with both feet stationary, and then executes two driving techniques into the lane for a layup.

1. On the left side a pivot is done on the left foot by swinging the right foot forward into the lane and driving for a layup.
2. A pivot may also be done on the right foot by dropping the left foot into the lane. The player slide-dribbles to the basket for a layup.

The same two driving maneuvers are accomplished from the right side of the floor.

Pivot to Baseline for the Jump Shot

Players divide into groups of three at a basket. One basketball is used. The same player positioning as in the previous drill is used. The ball is passed into the midpost on the left side. The receiver steps out to receive the ball with the left foot and extends the left hand as a target. After reception, a pivot is done on the right foot and the left foot swings toward the baseline to face the basket for a jump shot. After receiving five passes for jump shots, players rotate positions.

Pivot and Slide the Lane

The players divide into groups of three at a basket. One basketball is used. The players start in the same positions as in the previous post drills. The midpost player starts on the left side. The left foot and left hand are extended to receive the ball. After reception, the receiver slide-dribbles down the lane for a layup. Each player receives three passes before switching to the right side.

Variation: The midpost receives the ball with both feet stationary. Upon reception, the top foot is dropped into the lane and a slide dribble is executed to the basket for a layup.

Drive to Baseline and Reverse Pivot to Middle for Jump Shot

The squad divides into groups of four. Two players are assigned as passers with a basketball (A and B). One player (C) is the shooter in the midpost. Player D is the rebounder (Diagram 9-5). A starts by

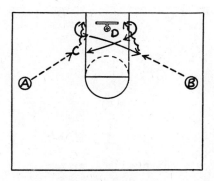

Diagram 9-5

passing to C. C dribbles down the lane to the baseline and pivots back to the middle for a jump shot. After the shot, C immediately moves across the lane and sets up in the midpost on the other side. Meanwhile, D has rebounded the first shot and passes back to A. B passes to C. C. dribbles down the lane to the baseline again and pivots back to the middle for a jump shot. C moves back and forth across the lane for a total of six shots. Players then switch positions.

Variation: Players attempt to make as many shots as possible in a thirty-second time period.

INDIVIDUAL OFFENSIVE MANEUVERS IN THE HIGH POST

The high post is located at the free throw line. All players should develop the necessary skills with their backs to the basket in the high post. A high-post player will be a screener, scorer, passer, and rebounder at different times depending upon the score and situation.

Drive the Lane

Players pair off at a basket with one basketball. One player stands in the high-post position with the back to the basket. The partner has a basketball outside the top of the key about twenty-five feet from the basket (Diagram 9-6).

The ball is passed into the high post. A variety of passes are thrown, including a bounce, chest, overhead, and underhand flip at different heights for difficulty in handling. The post receives the ball

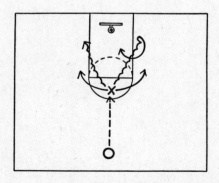

Diagram 9-6

with both feet stationary. After receiving the ball four pivot techniques are executed in driving to the basket:

1. A forward pivot on the right foot followed by a drive down the lane with a left hand dribble for a left-handed layup off the backboard.

2. A reverse pivot (drop step) with the right foot as the pivot foot and driving down the lane with the right hand for a right-handed layup off the dribble.

3. A forward pivot on the left foot followed by a drive down the lane with the right hand for a right-handed layup off the backboard.

4. A reverse pivot (drop step) with the left foot as the pivot foot and a drive down the lane with the left hand for a left-handed layup off the backboard.

After four passes, partners switch positions from offense to defense.

Slide the Lane

Players pair off at a basket with a basketball. One player stands in the high post with the back to the basket. The partner is outside the top of the key with a ball. The ball is passed into the high post with the back to the basket. The partner is outside the top of the key with a basketball. The ball is passed into the high post as outlined in the above drill. The ball is received with both feet stationary. Then a 90-degree drop step or reverse pivot is done into the lane so that the shoulder is pointing toward the basket. The player slides down the lane taking two or three dribbles to the basket for a layup. After two receptions driving right and left, partners switch positions.

Pivot and Square for Jump Shot

The players divide into groups of three at a basket with one ball. A is in the high post with the back to the basket. B is outside the top of the key with a basketball. C is the rebounder in the lane (Diagram 9-7).

Player B passes to A in the high post. A pivots to face the basket and takes a fifteen-foot jump shot. C rebounds and returns the ball to B. B may dribble around the perimeter from wing to wing and then passes the ball back into A. A receives five passes for jump shots. Players then rotate from A to B to C. The post player alternates turning left and right for jump shots.

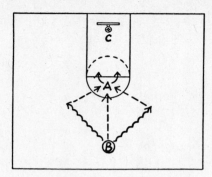

Diagram 9-7

PENETRATION

Dribbling penetration creates many offensive scoring possibilities. Splitting defenders forces the defense to make split-second
decisions on adjustments for coverage responsibilities. Consequently,
players will be left unguarded momentarily. Practicing the specific
skill of dribble penetration is essential to recognize the development
and take advantage of it when it occurs.

Two Across the lane

The squad lines up at half court with a ball. Two players (A and
B) are assigned to protect the lane. They stand even with the bottom
of the free throw circle. Their outside foot is on the lane line and their
inside arm extended across the lane (Diagram 9-8).

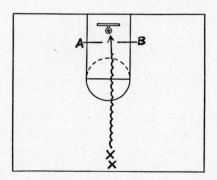

Diagram 9-8

Each player in turn starts dribbling and drives down the middle of the lane splitting the two defenders for a layup. The defense attempts to prevent a layup without fouling. After several opportunities, the defensive players switch. The offensive players rebound their own shot and return to the end of the line. Each time the players drive, they alternate penetrating and shooting with the left and right hand.

Dribble Drive Penetration

Organize the squad in two lines in a normal guard position at the top of the key. Three players are designated as defense (A-B-C) and are stationed across the free throw line evenly spaced apart (Diagram 9-9).

The first two players in line start passing the ball back and forth. When either player spots an opening between defenders, a dribble penetration is quickly attempted for a layup. Players return to opposite lines when the drill is completed. The defensive players remain and are switched after a period of time.

Variations: Stand out-of-bounds underneath the basket and indicate which offensive player will attempt to penetrate on the dribble.

A second variation is for you to stand behind the defense and designate the number of passes to be made before a dribble penetration is executed.

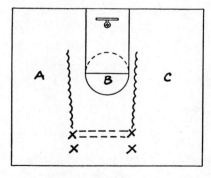

Diagram 9-9

10
Developing individual offensive techniques without the ball

Individual maneuvers without the ball are essential to becoming a complete offensive player. The most dangerous offensive player on the floor is the player who has just passed the ball. Offensive moves without the ball require awareness, alertness, recognition, and reaction to free a teammate or keep oneself open to become a potential scoring threat. The skills of setting a screen, changing direction, cutting, pivoting, and using a screen are effective offensive tools for the player without ball possession.

SETTING A SCREEN

Setting a proper screen is a fundamental to freeing a teammate with or without the basketball. The three types of screens to be learned and practiced are the rear screen, front screen, and side screen. Proper spacing and head-to-head alignment provides the largest screen possible to relieve defensive pressure and promote offensive scoring opportunities.

Proper Distance

The players spread out over the entire court. Two or three players are designated to start the drill simultaneously (Diagram 10-1). On your command, the designated players (A-E) move to any other player on the court and set a side screen with a two-foot jump stop. After checking position and spacing of the screen, sound another whistle. The two players who had a screen set on them move to set up a side screen on another player.

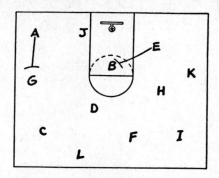

Diagram 10-1

Variations: The players set up rear screens concentrating on allowing enough distance for a normal step back to coincide with the basketball rule allowance.

The second variation is for the players to set up a front screen, which may be set as close as possible short of contact.

Always check position, balance, and head-head alignment before signaling new front screens to take place.

Screen and Roll

Divide the squad into two groups. Each group is assigned to a basket. A guard-guard and guard-forward situation is set up (Diagrams 10-2, 10-3). A passes to B and follows to screen. B starts dribbling off A's screen. A holds until B has dribbled by. A then rolls down the lane always facing the ball. B passes back to A for a layup. B follows for the rebound and taps in the shot if missed. The players switch positions after they execute a screen and roll maneuver.

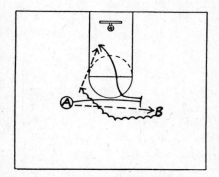

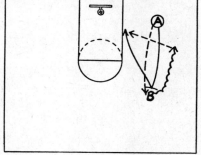

Diagram 10-2   *Diagram 10-3*

"L" Screen

Divide the squad into groups of four. The offense (A,B,C,D) lines up in a perimeter shell arrangement. The defense (1,2,3,4) lines up in normal defensive positioning on each player (Diagram 10-4).

Player A has the basketball and passes to B. A screens down for C. C moves up and replaces A. B passes to C and screens down for D. D moves up and replaces B. On every succeeding pass, the passer will screen away. If the pass goes from guard to forward, the guard screens across for the other guard. If the pass goes from forward to guard, the forward screens across the lane for the other forward. If the pass goes from guard to guard, the passer screens down the lane for the forward. The continuity of the drill continues for a specified period of time designated by you.

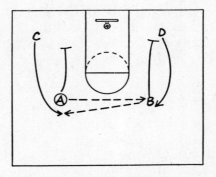

Diagram 10-4

Variation: Groups rotate at one basket from offense to defense and off the floor. The defense applies token resistance and must fight through the screens. It is important to check that screens are stationary and the proper position is established before movement occurs. It is advisable to employ a two-second count before moving off the screen.

Continuous Screen Away

Divide the squad into five player units. Each unit works at a separate basket. The players line up in a one-two-two formation to facilitate the continuity of movement (Diagram 10-5).

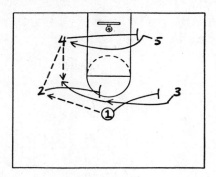

Diagram 10-5

The ball starts with player 1 in the point position. Player 1 passes to 2 and screens away for 3. Player 3 replaces 1 in the point position. Then 2 passes to 4 and screens away for 3. Player 3 replaces 2. Then 4 passes to 3 and screens across the lane for 5. The continuity of movement continues around the perimeter. Each pass is followed by a screen away and replacement of player to always have a one-two-two alignment.

> **Variation:** A defensive unit may be introduced to offer token resistance. Groups switch from offense to defense after a period of time.

FREEING MANEUVERS

Denfensive overplay to deny a pass dictates that players must learn how to counteract this pressure to receive a pass in an advantageous position to score. Offensive basketball is predicated on the ability of players to free themselves and get open.

In and Out

Divide the squad into groups of three at a basket. A is the passer. B is the receiver. C applies defensive pressure (Diagram 10-6). A has a basketball at the top of the free throw circle. B is lined up in a normal forward position which is halfway between the side line and foul lane. C is in an overplay defensive position. B steps toward C with the foot closest to the base line to force C to freeze. B then releases by stepping back with the outside foot in a long stride and extending the same hand as a target to receive a pass. A passes to the target. B then plays one-on-one against C until a basket is scored or C rebounds a missed shot. Players rotate from passer to offense to defense.

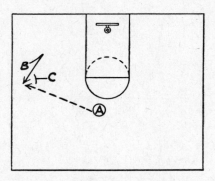

Diagram 10-6

Variations: The pass is made from guard to forward.
A second variation is to make the pass from guard to guard.
A third variation is to make the pass from forward to guard.

Step and Go

Divide the squad into groups of three at a basket. A is the passer. B is the receiver. C is the defensive player (Diagram 10-7). A has a basketball at the top of the free throw circle. B is on offense in a wing position. C is applying defensive pressure to B by overplaying to deny a direct pass in. B takes a short step toward A with the outside foot to draw the defense up. B immediately plays the same foot, pushes off to

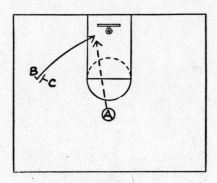

Diagram 10-7

change direction, and cuts to the basket behind the defense. A passes to B for a layup. Players rotate positions from offense to defense and off the floor.

Variations: The pass is made from the point to the right wing position.

A second variation is to make the pass from guard to guard.

A third variation is to make the pass from guard to forward on both sides of the floor.

Reverse and Dive

Divide the squad into groups of four at a basket. A, B, and C are on offense with a basketball. X is on defense guarding the passer (Diagram 10-8). A has a basketball in a guard position. X is guarding A and applying defensive pressure. B is lined up in the other guard position.C is lined up in a forward position on the side of the ball. A has the option to pass to either B or C. After the pass, C starts to screen away to the opposite player who received the pass. As C approaches midway between the base position and the player about to be screened, the outside foot is planted and a change of direction is initiated by reversing and cutting to the basket. The cut may be in front, (over the top of the defensive player) or behind the defensive player to receive a pass for a layup. Players will rotate from A to B to C to X after they have had two opportunities from each spot.

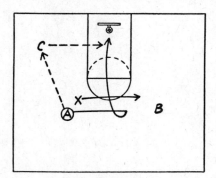

Diagram 10-8

Variations: The offensive players A, B, and C are set up in a point-wing-forward alignment. A second variation is for the offensive players to line up in a point-wing-wing situation.

CUTTING

Proper cutting is an effective and productive offensive technique for the player without the ball. Execution is based on timing, balance, and proper footwork to change direction and accelerate as efficiently as possible. Creating scoring opportunities as well as catching the ball on the move are essential offensive skills.

"V" Cuts

The squad divides into two lines at one basket. A is lined up outside the end line with the first player on the juncture of the baseline and foul lane. B is lined up on the opposite wing with a basketball (Diagram 10-9). B bounces the basketball once to initiate A's movement. A moves straight up the foul lane to the free throw line. Upon reaching the juncture, A pushes off with the outside foot and a "V" cut is taken back to the basket receiving a pass for a layup. B follows and rebounds the shot. A and B switch lines. The drill is executed from both sides of the floor with concentration on moving up in a straight line, planting the outside (top) foot, pushing off, and accelerating on a 45-degree angle back toward the basket to receive a pass.

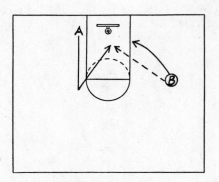

Diagram 10-9

"L" Cuts

Divide the squad into two lines at one basket. The cutting line A lines up on the sideline opposite the free throw line. The passing line B lines up on the opposite baseline in the corner (Diagram 10-10). B bounces a basketball to initiate A's movement. A starts by cutting across the free throw line. When A reaches the juncture of the foul lane and free throw line, the foot is planted which is farthest from the basket. In a right angle change of direction, A pushes off and accelerates down the lane to receive a pass from B for a layup. A and B switch lines after cutting and passing. The drill is run from both sides of the floor. Concentration is on moving in a straight line, making a right angle cut in balance, and accelerating in a straight line down the lane to the basket.

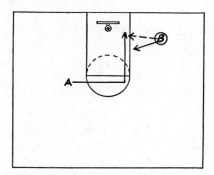

Diagram 10-10

"I" Cuts

Divide the squad into lines at one basket. Line A is on the sideline even with the bottom of the free throw circle. Line B is stationed out-of-bounds on the end line even with the foul lane (Diagram 10-11). B starts with a basketball in the low-post position with the back to the basket B passses to A on the sideline. B slides up

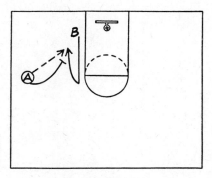

Diagram 10-11

the lane until hitting the juncture of the foul lane and free throw line. Immediately B reverses by planting the top foot and pushing off to move back down the lane to receive a pass for a power layup. B reverses so that the ball is always faced on the way back to the basket. A maximum of one dribble is allowed after the reception. A rebounds the shot and passes out quickly to the sideline. A and B switch lines. The drill is run from both sides of the court after each player has made three "I" cuts for layups.

BACKDOOR CUTTING MANEUVER

The backdoor cut is one of the most effective offensive maneuvers in basketball. For easy baskets, the element of surprise forces the defense to ease up on overplay defensive pressure because of the potential consequences. All players must learn the backdoor cut and develop the ability to recognize the opportunity when it becomes available.

Jab Step and Cut Behind

Divide the squad into two lines. Line A has basketballs at the top of the key. Line B is stationed on the sideline in a normal wing position. You or a manager stands in an overplay defensive position on B to simulate game conditions (Diagram 10-12). A starts by dribbling three times in place. After the third dribble the ball is picked up. B jab steps toward A with the right foot. Immediately upon planting the foot, B pushes off and reverses direction. B cuts behind the defense and continues to the basket for a layup after receiving a

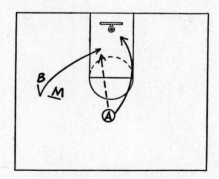

Diagram 10-12

pass from A. A follows for the rebound. A and B switch lines. After each player has cut three times from the left side, the cutting line is switched to the right side.

Variations: The same backdoor cut is executed with the guard and forward working together.

A. The forward cuts with the guard passing (Diagram 10-13).

B. The guard cuts with the forward passing (Diagram 10-14).

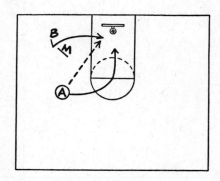

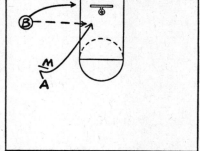

Diagram 10-13   Diagram 10-14

It is absolutely necessary for both the passer and receiver to communicate and know when the backdoor cut can be effective. The receiver may signal when a cut is anticipated. One excellent method is for the receiver to extend the outside hand to receive a pass. Instead of having the palm open as in establishing a target to receive a direct pass, the first is closed, which indicates to the passer a backdoor cut is going to be made. This little technique will help to improve timing and eliminate hesitation or misinformation resulting in turnovers.

GIVE-AND-GO MANEUVER

Passing and cutting will always be one of the most effective scoring maneuvers. Faking a screening situation sets the defense up for a give-and-go situation to receive a return pass for a score. In many cases, the defense does not anticipate the cutting action and the result is an easy basket for the defense.

Guard-Forward Exchange

Divide the squad into two lines. Line A has basketballs and lines up in a normal guard position. Line B is set up in a normal offensive forward position. A manager is set up in a defensive position anticipating a screen away from the ball (Diagram 10-15). A passes to B. A starts as if screening away from the ball. As A approaches the manager, a push is taken off the outside foot, and A cuts straight down the middle of the lane in front of the manager for a return pass from B for a layup. B follows for the rebound. A and B switch lines. After each player cuts three times moving from left to right, the drill is switched to the other side of the floor.

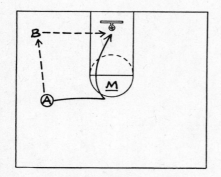

Diagram 10-15   Diagram 10-16

Variation: Guard to guard pass and screening down for the forward (Diagram 10-16).

A passes to B and starts to screen down. As A approaches the manager, a push is taken off the outside foot and acceleration achieved into the lane for a return pass and layup. B follows for the rebound. After each player has cut three times working on the left side of the floor, the drill is switched to the right side.

RUB-OFF MANEUVER

Passing and cutting off a screen to rub off the defensive player increases the chances of getting a layup. The techique of running a defensive player into a screen must be practiced to develop timing and proper spacing of the players to be effective.

Point Cut

Divide the squad into three lines at one basket. B and C are in normal wing positions on either side of the floor. A is on the top of the key with a basketball. A manager or other player is positioned on the free throw line (Diagram 10-17).

A passes to B or C. After a quick head fake, A cuts down the middle of the lane off X to receive a pass back for a layup. The opposite wing follows for the rebound and clears the ball out. The rebounder dribbles the ball back to the middle line. The shooter moves to the end of the line from which the pass was received. The passing wing moves through the lane to the end of the line on the opposite wing.

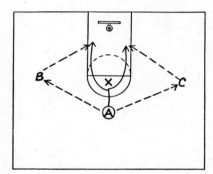   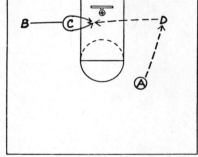

Diagram 10-17   *Diagram 10-18*

Baseline Cut

Divide the squad into two lines. Line A is in a normal guard position on the right side of the lane. Line B is lined up on the baseline in the corner. One player (C) is the permanent screener and is stationed in the low-post position on the left side. Another player (D) is the permanent passer in the right corner (Diagram 10-18).

A passes to D. B cuts off C to receive a pass from D for a layup. Line B alternates cutting over the top of C and on the baseline side to receive the pass. A rebounds the shot. A and B then switch lines. After all the players have taken a baseline cut, C and D are replaced by two other players. The drill is then switched to the other side of the floor.

Wing Cut

The squad lines up in a normal wing position on the left side of the floor. Players B,C, and D are stationed at the top of the key, on the opposite wing, and as a screener on the juncture of the foul lane and free throw line (Diagram 10-19).

A passes to B. B passes to C. A fakes and cuts off screener D to receive a pass from C for a layup. A rebounds the shot and then moves to the position of C. C moves to line B. B goes to the end of line A. D remains as the screener. After all the players have cut off the wing for a layup, another player is selected to replace D. The drill is switched to the right side of the floor after all the players have cut to the basket three times.

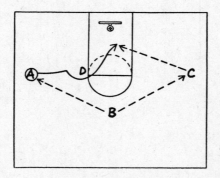

Diagram 10-19

PICK AND ROLL

The pick and roll technique is an explosive offensive weapon. The ability to set a screen, use a screen, pass and receive the basketball in close proximity is the essence of offensive basketball. Practice devoted to these skills is essential for all players to develop timing for the pick and roll maneuver.

Forward Screening Guard

Divide the squad into four lines at one basket (A-B-C-D). A and B are in the normal guard position while C and D have basketballs in the normal forward positions (Diagram 10-20).

C passes to A and moves up to screen. A drives off the screen toward the baseline. As A moves by C, C rolls down the lane to the basket and receives a pass back for a layup. A follows to rebound the shot. A and C switch lines. As soon as A and C clear the lane, B and D on the other side of the floor start to perform the same action. After the players have executed the drill three times on their respective side of the floor, they switch to the opposite side.

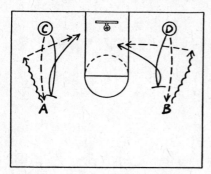
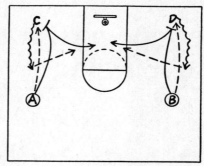

Diagram 10-20   *Diagram 10-21*

Guard Screening Forward

Divide the squad into four lines at one basket. Guards A and B have a basketball while C and D are stationed in a normal forward position (Diagram 10-21).

A passes to C and follows to screen. C dribbles off the screen and looks for A rolling into the lane. C passes to A for a shot and follows to rebound. A and C switch lines. As soon as A and C clear the lane, B and D execute the same maneuver. After the players have executed the drill three times on their respective side of the floor, they switch to the opposite side.

11
Developing team offensive skills and techniques

In order to develop an effective team offense, it is essential that offensive maneuvers be established within the framework of your offensive philosophy. All offensive situations involving the ball directly relate to two-, three-, or four-player situations with options occurring based on the action or reaction of the defensive players. Consequently, it is important to concentrate on and emphasize offensive breakdown situations in the early stages of learning to develop performance efficiency.

Discipline, control, and patience are equally important as factors in developing theories of offensive play. The building blocks are firmly established in a progressive sequence from two-, three-, and four-player involvement before implementing the total offense involving five players.

RULES OF PLAY

All scrimmage situations should include control factors to improve execution, concentration, and effective effort. The factors in force will vary depending on the situation and objectives or goals.

Maneuver Execution

Each offensive series in the breakdown concept begins with the offense executing a specific maneuver before attempting to score. Repetition is the key to learning. Failure to execute properly results in loss of possession.

Score Conditions

When situations involve both offense and defense, some form of scorekeeping is essential to improving effort, execution, and output. Players are interested in the win-loss concept and work harder and more carefully when scoring is meaningful.

Time-Limit Restrictions

All players should be kept active in a game-type situation at different baskets. This allows a maximum amount of time for all players to improve. All groups begin and finish together to keep within the allotted practice time. The daily practice session should not be disrupted due to inefficient planning time.

Basket Out Emphasis

An excellent method to emphasize offensive execution and good shot selection is to incorporate the basket out rule. By scoring, the offensive team retains possession for the next offensive series.

Passing Limitations

Placing limitations on passing will encourage concentration. Players must think first before looking to pass or score.

Delivering the wrong type of pass results in play stoppage and loss of possession. Emphasize bounce passes for a period of time and make them the only type of pass allowed in the scrimmage. Likewise, emphasize chest passes and allow only them during different phase of the scrimmage. Overhead passes should also be stressed during certain periods of time. Emphasis on mastering the three basic pass options aids in ball control and minimizes turnover possibilities.

Dribble Restrictions

Overdribbling can be controlled or eliminated by restricting the number of dribbles each player may use. No more then three consecutive dribbles on each possession should be allowed in the four-on-four games. Four dribbles should be the maximum per possession in the three-on-three games. In the two-on-two games a total of five dribbles may be used before a pass must occur.

Shooting Restrictions

Individual shooting range can be aided by placing shooting limitations on the players:

1. No shots taken beyond the free throw line.
2. Shots may be taken only inside the free throw lane.
3. Layups only are allowed.
4. Jump shots outside the lane are allowed only after a specified number of passes have been made.

Percentage Score Opportunities

The offensive team receives three to five opportunities to score. By converting a designated percentage established by you, the offensive team receives another series to score.

TWO-ON-TWO COMPETITION

Two-player situations are the cornerstone to developing offensive team play. All offensive series or plays involve at least two players. One player having ball possession and at least one other player are involved to help initiate the offensive thrust. Two-player alignments include guard-guard, guard-forward, guard-post, forward-post, point-wing, point-post, and wing-post. Each series to score is initiated by a specific maneuver designated to develop offensive continuity.

Pass and Screen the Ball

Organize players into pairs. Assign three pairs of players to a basket. Pair A is on offense. Pair B is on defense. Pair C is off the court ready to move into play. Pair A sets up offensively in a formation designated by you. Pair B matches up defensively (Diagram 11-1). A1 passes to A2 and follows to set a screen. After the initial entry maneuver, the offense and defense play two-on-two until a basket is scored or the defense rebounds. On each succeeding offensive series, the pass-and-screen ball maneuver must be executed before attempting to score. The rotation of groups is from offense to defense and off the court.

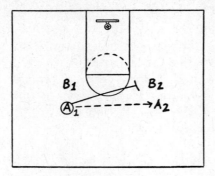

Diagram 11-1

Variations: The offensive team remains on offense while scoring. The other two groups alternate defensively.

A second variation is to have the defensive unit remain on defense until they stop the offense from scoring. The other two groups alternate offensively.

Pass and Cut

Organize players into pairs. Three pairs are assigned to a basket. Pair A is on offense and sets up in a guard-guard alignment. Team B is on defense. Team C is off the court (Diagram 11-2).

A1 passes to A2 and cuts to the basket. After the initial cutting maneuver, a two-on-two game is played until the offense scores or the defense rebounds a missed shot. Each time a basket is scored, the offense must start by passing and cutting to the basket to initiate the next series.

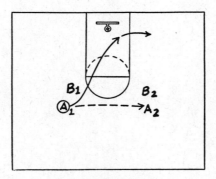

Diagram 11-2

Variations: Games are played for three baskets. The team scoring retains possession (basket out). Games are played for three minutes. The ball switches teams on a score.

Another variation is for the team scoring to remain on offense while the other two teams alternate defensively.

A final variation is for the defensive unit to stay on defense until they stop the offense from scoring. The other two teams alternate offensively.

Pass and Post Up Low

Organize players into pairs. Assign three pairs of players to a basket. Pair A is on offense and sets up in a point-wing alignment. Pair B is matched up on defense. Pair C is waiting off the court (Diagram 11-3).

The point passes to the wing and cuts to the basket. After completing the cut, the point moves to the low-post ball side and posts up to receive a pass. The ball is delivered from the wing position. After the initial pass, a two-on-two game is played. Each time a basket is scored, the next offensive series must be started from a point-wing alignment.

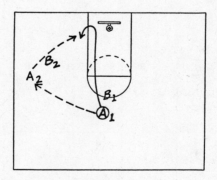

Diagram 11-3

Variations: Games are played for three baskets. The team scoring retains possession (basket out). Games are played for three minutes. The ball switches teams on a score.

Another variation is for the team scoring to remain on offense while the other two teams alternate defensively.

A final variation is for the defensive unit to stay on defense until they stop the offense from scoring. The other two teams alternate offensively.

Dribble Off a Screen

Assign three pairs of players to a basket. Pair A is on offense and sets up in a guard-guard or guard-forward alignment (Diagram 11-4). A1 passes to A2 and sets a screen. A2 dribbles off the screen to initiate a two-on-two game against pair B. Each time a basket is scored, the offense must start again by initiating a dribble off a screen maneuver before playing two-on-two.

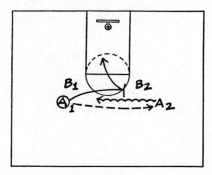

Diagram 11-4

Variations: A game is played for three baskets with the team scoring retaining possession.

A second variation is for the ball to switch teams on a score and the game to be played for three minutes.

A third variation is for two teams to alternate defensively as the offensive team continues to score.

A fourth variation is for two teams to alternate offensively until the defense stops the offense from scoring.

THREE-ON-THREE COMPETITION

Three-player situations help develop both the ballside and offside offensive play. Involving three players in an offensive series incorporates passing, cutting, and screening maneuvers, which are key elements in any offensive pattern. Three-play alignments include point-wing-wing, guard-guard-high post, guard-forward-high post, guard-forward-low post, and point-wing-forward.

Pass and Screen the Ball

Divide the squad into groups of three. Assign two groups to a basket. The offensive team sets up in a point-wing-wing alignment (Diagram 11-5).

The ball starts in the point position. The ball is passed to either wing to start play. The passser follows and sets a screen. After the initial entry maneuver, the teams play a three-on-three game. After each score, the ball is started again from the point position with the original pass and screen maneuver completed before playing three-on-three.

Variations: A game is played for three baskets with the team scoring retaining possession.

A second variation is to play the game for three minutes with the ball switching teams after a score.

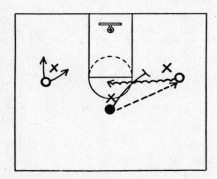

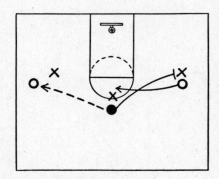

Diagram 11-5   Diagram 11-6

Pass and Screen Away

Divide the squad into groups of three. Assign two groups to a basket. The offensive team sets up in a point-wing-wing alignment (Diagram 11-6).

The ball starts in the point position and is passed to either wing to start play. After passing, the point moves away and screens for the opposite wing. A three-on-three game is played until the offense scores or the defense gains possession. Each succeeding offensive series starts from the original setup with the pass and screen away maneuver before playing three-on-three.

Variations: A game is played for three baskets with the team scoring retaining possession.

A second variation is to play the game for three minutes with the ball switching teams after a score.

Pass and Cut

Divide the squad into groups of three. Assign two groups to a basket. The offensive team sets up in a point-wing-wing alignment (Diagram 11-7).

The ball starts in the point position and is passed to either wing to start play. After passing, the point cuts to the basket looking for a return pass. After the cut is completed, a three-on-three game is played until the offense scores or the defense gains possession. Each succeeding offensive series starts from the original setup with the pass and cut maneuver before playing three-on-three.

Variations: A game is played for three baskets with the team scoring retaining possession.

A second variation is to play the game for three minutes with the ball switching teams after a score.

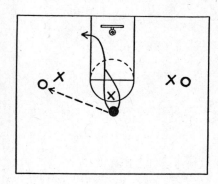

Diagram 11-7

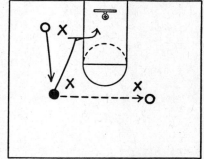

Diagram 11-8

Downscreen and Post Up

Divide the squad into groups of three. Two groups are assigned to a basket. The offensive team sets up in a guard-guard-forward alignment (Diagram 11-8). The ball starts in the guard position on the same side as the forward. Play is initiated by a guard-to-guard pass. After passing, the guard screens down for the forward. The forward moves off the screen and the guard reverses into the lane looking for a pass. After the initial offensive maneuver is completed, the teams play three-on-three until the offense scores or the defense gains possession. Each succeeding offensive series starts from the original setup with the offensive maneuver completed before the three-on-three action.

Variations: A game is played for three baskets with the team scoring retaining possession.

A second variation is to play the game for three minutes with the ball switching teams after a score.

Dribble Off a Screen and a Backdoor Cut

Divide the squad into groups of three. Assign two groups to a basket. The offensive team sets up in a guard-guard-forward alignment (Diagram 11-9).

The ball starts in the guard position on the same side as the forward. Play is initiated by a guard-to-guard pass. After passing, G1 screens across for G2. G2 starts dribbling off the screen across the top of the key. As G2 approaches the key, the forward fakes toward the ball and immediately cuts to the basket looking for a pass. After the initial offensive maneuver is completed, a three-on-three game is played. After every score, the ball starts in the original position with the offensive maneuver being completed before the three-on-three continues.

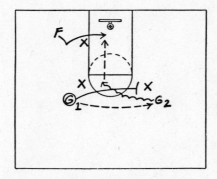

Diagram 11-9

Variations: A game is played for three baskets with the team scoring retaining possession.

A second variation is to play the game for three minutes with the ball switching teams after a score.

When there is an odd number of team players, the extra player is assigned to a basket. The player substitutes at the conclusion of each offensive series. The substitute replaces the player who misses and causes loss of team possession.

FOUR-ON-FOUR COMPETITION

The crux of offensive basketball is developed on four-on-four play. As the individual offensive techniques improve, four-on-four introduces floor balance and post play into the offensive team concept. This allows for greater offensive flexibility and option selection. Team involvement becomes primary as an outgrowth from concentration on individual offensive maneuvers. Offensive alignments include guard-guard-forward-forward, point-wing-forward-high post, point-wing-forward-low post, point-wing-wing-high post, guard-forward-low post-high post.

Pass and Screen the Ball

Divide the squad into groups of four. Three groups are at the same basket. Offensive group A sets up in a two-guard and two-forward alignment. Defensive group B is matched up. Group C is off the court ready to move on (Diagram 11-10).

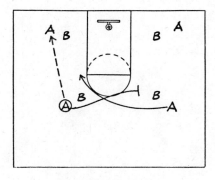

Diagram 11-10

The ball starts in either guard position. Play starts with a pass to the opposite guard or the forward on the ball side. The passer follows and screens for the receiver. After the entry pass and subsequent screen, the groups play four-on-four until the offense scores or the defense rebounds a missed shot. After each score, the ball starts in the original position with the offensive maneuver being completed before the four-on-four continues.

Variations: A game is played to three baskets with the team scoring retaining possession.

A game is played for three minutes with the ball switching teams after a score.

A third variation is to rotate from offense to defense and off the court after each offensive series is completed.

When there is an odd number of players, make substitutions at the conclusion of each offensive series. The substitute replaces the player who misses the shot and causes loss of possession.

Pass and Cut

Three units of four players are assigned to a basket. The offensive unit sets up in a two-guard and two-forward alignment. The defensive unit is assigned matchups. The third group is off the court ready to move into play quickly (Diagram 11-11).

Play starts with the ball being passed from guard to guard, guard to ballside forward, or guard to opposite forward flashing into the lane as a post player. After the pass has been received, the passer immediately cuts to the basket looking for a return pass. The cutter then clears the lane to the ball side. After the initial cut, a four-on-

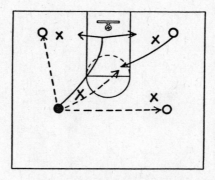

Diagram 11-11

four game is played until the offense scores or the defense gains possession of the ball. Each subsequent offensive series begins with a pass and cut maneuver. Extra players substitute for the player missing a shot at the conclusion of the series.

Variations: A game is played to three baskets with the team scoring retaining possession.

A game is played for three minutes with the ball switching teams after a score.

A third variation is to rotate from offense to defense and off the court after each offensive series is completed.

Downscreen and Post Up

Assign three units of four players to a basket. The offensive unit sets up in a two-guard and two-forward alignment. Defensive matchups are assigned for group two. The third group is off the court. The ball starts in either guard position. The opposite guard screens down for the forward to move up and receive a pass. The screener immediately reverses and posts up low looking for the ball. On the other side of the floor, the guard screens down for the forward after making the first pass. Three passes are completed with the resulting screening action taking place before the groups scrimmage. Play is stopped after the offense scores or the defense gains possession of the ball. Each offensive series is initiated with three pass exchanges before the offense and defense go full out (Diagram 11-12).

Variations: A game is played to three baskets with the team scoring retaining possession.

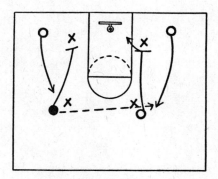

Diagram 11-12

A game is played for three minutes with the ball switching teams after a score.

A third variation is to rotate from offense to defense and off the court after each offensive series is completed.

Dribble Off with a Backdoor Cut and Pop-Out Maneuver

Assign three units of four players to a basket. The offensive unit sets up in a two-guard and two-forward alignment. Assign defensive matchups (Diagram 11-13).

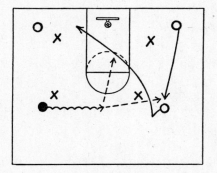

Diagram 11-13

The ball starts in either guard position. Play starts with the guard dribbling across the top of the key toward the other guard. As the dribbler approaches, the guard fakes and breaks backdoor to the basket looking for a pass. After the cut has been completed a four-on-four scrimmage is played until a basket is scored or the defense gains possession. Each subsequent offensive series begins in the same fashion. Additional players are substituted for the player missing the shot before the next series begins.

Variations: A game is played to three baskets with the team scoring retaining possession.

A game is played for three minutes with the ball switching teams after a score.

A third variation is to rotate from offense to defense and off the court after each offensive series is completed.

Flashing Post Maneuver

Assign three units of four players to a basket. The offensive unit lines up in a two-guard and two-forward alignment. Assign defensive matchups. The third group is waiting off the court (Diagram 11-14).

The ball starts in either guard position. Three pass exchanges are made between the guards. On each pass, the opposite forward flashes into the lane looking for a pass. During the three passes, the defensive forwards contest the flash-post maneuver. The defensive guards allow the passes back and forth. After the three passes are completed, both units play full go until the offense scores or the defense gains possession. At any time during the three-pass exchange, the guards can pass the ball into the post if open. Once the ball is received by the post, play is full go. Each subsequent offensive series is initiated by the guard-to-guard pass exchanges.

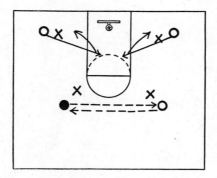

Diagram 11-14

Variations: Each team receives three opportunities on offense. If they convert at least two opportunities, they receive another series on offense.

A second variation is to play a three-basket game with the team scoring retaining possession.

A third variation is to play a three-minute game with the ball switching teams after a score.

A fourth variation is to rotate from offense to defense and off the court after each offensive series is completed.

Pass and Screen Exchange

Assign three units of four players to a basket. The offense lines up in a two-guard and two-forward alignment. Defensive matchups are assigned to group two. The third group is waiting on the sideline (Diagram 11-15).

The ball starts in either guard position. Four passes are made with the screen exchange action taking place before any attempt to score. The following sequence is used to involve all the offensive players in a screening situation: Guard 1 passes to forward 1 and screens across for guard 2. Forward 1 passes to guard 2 and screens across for forward 2. Guard 2 passes to guard 1 and screens down for forward 2. Guard 1 passes to forward 1 and screens across for forward 2. After the four passes, a four-on-four scrimmage is played until the offense scores or the defense gains possession. Each subsequent offensive series is initiated by the four pass exchanges.

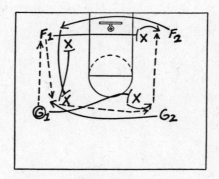

Diagram 11-15

Variations: Each team receives three opportunities on offense. If they convert at least two opportunities, they receive another series on offense.

A second variation is to play a three-basket game with the team scoring retaining possession.

A third variation is to play a three-minute game with the ball switching teams after a score.

A fourth variation is to rotate from offense to defense and off the court after each offensive series is completed.

12
Improving game shooting proficiency

Basketball is the longest sport season on the high school and college level of play. The length of time requires constant adjustments, innovations, and imagination when structuring practice sessions to keep a team at the peak of their game.

Boredom may easily become a problem created by the constant repetition of the same drills day after day regardless of how "super" a drill may be. Staleness becomes a major concern when players are unchallenged and no provision for variety is incorporated into the practice organization. Momentum can become nonexistent if the players are not extended and special techniques for improving team success are not developed. Details and something "extra" are needed to motivate players.

Certain game situations lend themselves to the "big play" concept, which can create instant momentum. All of these concepts must be taken into consideration and incorporated into both the long- and short-term organization to minimize the factors that will interfere with the learning process. In particular, shooting proficiency will only improve if shooting drills incorporate speed and/or pressure factors that are constant elements in a game.

INTENTIONALLY MISSED FREE THROW

Many times in the closing seconds of a game, missing a free throw on purpose will be advantageous to the offense. Practice must include this important phase on a regular basis. The free throw must be developed to a degree where it resembles a definite attempt at making it so that the defense will not be tipped off on the intention of missing.

Partners Shoot One-One

Squad members are paired off at all available baskets. Partners alternate turns shooting a one-one free throw attempt. Each partner in turn steps to the free throw line with a basketball. A one-one is attempted. The first free throw is made and the second is missed intentionally. The partner is lined up in the second lane position ready to rebound the miss. On the intentional miss, an attempt is made to tap the ball in. When attempting to miss a free throw intentionally, it's important to remember:

1. The shot must always resemble a normal free throw attempt.
2. Extra velocity must be added to the shot by increasing the wrist extension on the release. The ball must hit the rim to be in play.

Three-Player Rotation

Divide the squad into groups of three. Partners alternate shooting a one-one free throw attempt. Each player in turn steps to the free throw line with a ball. The other two players line up in the second lane positions opposite each other. The shooter makes the first free throw and misses the second shot intentionally, but makes sure the ball hits the rim. Rebounders attempt to tap the ball in.

Variation: Increase competition by having the player who taps in the missed shot go to the free throw line next. One is a defensive rebounder in the first lane position while the other is an offensive rebounder in the second lane position.

Five-Player Competition

Split the squad into five player units. Two units line up in an offensive and defensive free throw shooting arrangement. The offensive unit receives five opportunities at the free throw line with each player rotating to the free throw line. Each player shoots a one-one. The first free throw is made. The second is missed intentionally. If the offense misses the first shot of the one-one, they run. Substitutions are made after both units have shot and switched.

CONVERTING THREE-POINT PLAYS

The most satisfying offensive maneuver is scoring a three-point play. This is a great psychological advantage for the offense at any time during the game. Drills can be developed in practice to give the players the feel of scoring a basket and making a subsequent free throw to complete a three-point play.

Three-Player Scramble

Divide the squad into groups of four. Assign each group to a basket. One basketball is used per group. Three of the players stand inside the lane facing the basket. The fourth player has the basketball at the free throw line (Diagram 12-1).

The shooter takes a jump shot from the free throw line. As long as the shots are made, the player continues moving around the perimeter and shooting. On a miss, the three lane players fight for the rebound and immediately power up to make a shot through the inevitable contact of the other two. The player scoring moves to the free throw line and shoots a free throw to complete the three-point play. If the free throw is made, the player becomes the perimeter jump shooter. If the free throw is missed, the lane players rebound and power the ball back up for a layup. A game can be played among the four players. The score is kept individually with one point for a made jump shot, two points for a rebound basket, and three points for a completed three-point play.

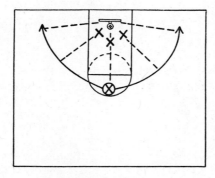

Diagram 12-1

TEAM SHOOTING COMPETITION

Concentration and competition are essential to improving shooting skill. Devise shooting games for practice. This will increase pressure and motivate players to concentrate harder. Establish goals for players to succeed and have some fun at the same time while making the shooting phase of practice productive.

Pressure Jump Shooting

Divide the squad into two teams. Designate the teams or select two players to choose sides. Both teams line up at the same basket. They line up on either side of the lane at the juncture of the free throw line. One basketball is used for each team (Diagram 12-2).

On your signal, the first player from each team shoots a jump shot and follows to rebound. The ball is passed to the next player in line while the first player returns to the end of the line. The first team to make eleven baskets wins. A basket is subtracted each time a player interferes with the other team's ball when rebounding. The losing team is assigned a sprint or has a challenge option available for a double or nothing chance.

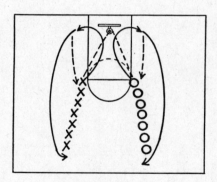

Diagram 12-2

Variations: The teams play a two out of three match and switch sides after each game.

A second variation is that each player must rebound the shot before it hits the floor or the basket does not count.

A third variation is for teams to shoot from opposite corners on the baseline.

Partner's Tournament

Divide the squad into two player teams. Several different methods may be employed to select teams. Each team has a ball and is assigned to a basket at the free throw line. On a signal from you, all teams start together. One partner starts by shooting a jump shot and follows in to rebound. The ball is immediately passed back to the partner at the free throw line. Partners continue alternating and shooting. Games are played to eleven baskets or the number of baskets made in a specific time period.

Variations: Two teams are assigned to a basket. A round robin tournament is played.

A second variation is to assign two teams to a basket and run a single elimination tournament for winners and losers.

Scramble Layups

Divide the squad into groups of four players. Stand in the lane underneath the basket. Players in the group stand behind a chair at midcourt (Diagram 12-3).

Start by tossing the basketballs to one side or the other. The first player in line responds by sprinting to the basketball, recovering, and dribbling in for a layup. Meanwhile, the second player has moved in to pick up the other ball. After players shoot, they immediately run back to half court around the chair and get ready to move in again. They never touch the ball after the shot. The drill continues until the group makes twenty-five layups in a row.

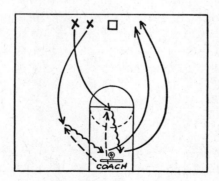

Diagram 12-3

Scramble Jump Shooting

Divide the squad into groups of three or four players. Two basketballs are used. You or a manager stands in the lane under the basket with both basketballs. All players in the group stand behind a chair at midcourt (Diagram 12-4).

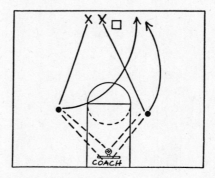

Diagram 12-4

You start the drill by dropping a ball off to the side outside the line. The first player in line sprints to recover the ball, takes one dribble to gain balance, and moves into shooting range for a jump shot outside the foul lane. The second ball is dropped to the other side of the basket by you. The next player in line moves after the loose ball and recovers it to take a jump shot. As soon as the players shoot they immediately turn and run back behind the chair before moving back in to recover another ball. Two balls are continuously being recovered. If the shot is made, you catch the ball and throw it to a new position on the floor for the next player to recover. If a shot is missed, the next player sprints to recover the ball wherever it has rebounded. The drill continues until the group has made twenty-five jump shots. While the drill is being conducted at one basket, the other players are shooting free throws, layups, and working on dribble maneuvers at the other available baskets.

Overtake Layups

Divide the squad into two teams (A and B). Half the players on each team are on opposite end lines underneath the baskets (Diagram 12-5).

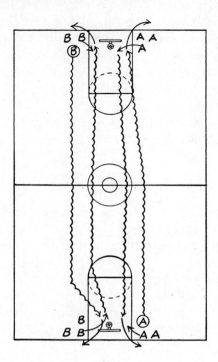

Diagram 12-5

One basketball is used by each team. The ball is in possession of A and B at opposite ends. On your signal, A and B start driving toward the opposite basket as fast as possible to make a layup. Nobody is allowed to touch the ball until the layup is made. The next player in line grabs the ball and drives back for a layup. Lines A and B continuously drive back and forth shooting layups and going to the end of their respective lines. The game continues until one team passes the other team going in the same direction and makes a layup.

Variations: Players shoot right-hand layups only.

A second variation is for players to shoot left-hand layups only.

Overtake Jump Shots

Divide the squad into two teams. As in the above layup drill, half the players on each team are sent to either end line underneath the basket. The same procedure is followed. Basketballs start with the teams at opposite ends. Each player in turn dribbles as fast as possible to the opposite free throw line and takes a jump shot. If the shot is made, the next player in line grabs the ball and dribbles to the opposite free throw line for a jump shot. If the shot is missed, the shooter must rebound the shot. The ball is dribbled outside the lane to the left or right of the basket and a jump shot is taken off the backboard. The players continue doing this until the shot is made. The game continues until one team passes the other team going in the same direction and makes a jump shot.

Basket Elimination

The entire squad is lined up one behind another at the free throw line of a basket. Each player has a ball. One after another, each player shoots a jump shot and follows for the rebound. If the jump shot is made, the player goes to the end of the line at the same basket. If the shot is missed, the player moves to the next basket on the right. The same procedure is followed at each of the six baskets moving to the next one on a miss. The last player remaining who has not missed any of the six baskets is the winner.

INDIVIDUAL SHOOTING COMPETITION

Shooting drills must be designed to emphasize specific types of shots taken from specific areas on the floor. This develops concentration and awareness for shooting spots. Shot selection and individual shooting range will be learned by the players to apply in games with confidence.

Hook Shot—Layup Competition

Squad members pair off at a basket with one ball. Each partner in turn will attempt to make the greatest number of consecutive layups and/or hook shots in a row. A time limit is imposed to stop all groups together. Winners pair off in a championship bracket. Losers pair off in a consolation bracket. Players are ranked in order of their performance. Some form of sprinting or penalty is awarded in reverse order with the top three shooters excused.

Jump Shooting Competition

Squad members pair off at a basket with one ball. Five perimeter areas are designated as shooting spots (right corner, left corner, right wing, left wing, top of the key). Partners shoot against each other from the five spots at a distance of fifteen feet. The winner is determined by the player making the most shots out of ten from each specific spot.

Variations: The winners are determined by the most consecutive shots made from each spot.

A second variation is to declare the winner as the player who made the most at three of the five spots. The losers may be assigned extra sprints or be required to remain after practice to make a designated percentage of shots at the spots where unsuccessful.

Backboard Shooting Competition

Squad members pair off at a basket with one basketball. Six shooting spots are marked off on the foul lane (Diagram 12-6).

Partners alternate turns shooting from each spot using the backboard only. The partner making the most consecutive bank shots or the most bank shots out of a specific number is the winner. All six spots are contested in the same fashion. The winner of the most spots is the champion. If the six spots are tied 3-3, players alternate free throws in a sudden death shoot-off.

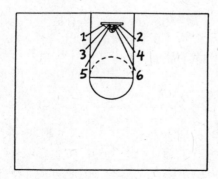

Diagram 12-6

Free Throw Shooting Competition

Squad members pair off at a basket with one ball. Each partner in turn goes to the free throw line. Several methods are used to develop the competitive edge in free throw shooting:

1. Partners attempt to make as many free throws in a row as possible. Each player shoots until making the first free throw and then continues shooting until missing.
2. Partners shoot a specific number of free throws and record the total made to determine the winner.
3. Players match free throws alternating shooting one at a time.
4. Partners continue matching free throws until one player has a three-shot advantage.

Match Competition

Players compete in pairs at a basket. Each player has a choice for three consecutive shots. The partner must follow suit. Example: A makes shot one; B misses. A is one up. A makes shot two; B also makes. A is still one up. A misses shot three; B makes the shot. The match is even. B then leads for three shots.

Variations: A game is played until one player is five shots ahead.
A second variation is to give each player three sets of shots. The player ahead at the end is the winner.
A third variation is to play a five-minute game.

Number in a Row

Players pair off at a basket with one ball. Each partner in turn shoots a specific shot until one is made and then continues shooting until missing. The object is to make the most number of shots in a row. Partners alternate turns selecting the shooting spot.

Variations: The winner of the competition is the first player winning three spots.
A second variation is to play a time limit game.

Letter Game

Place players in groups of three. The order of players shooting is determined by matching free throws. The player shooting first may select a shot from any area. If made, succeeding players must attempt the same shot. A letter is awarded if missed. When a shot is missed, the next player in the shooting order selects the new spot and shot.

Variations: A three-letter "pig" is played.
A second variation is to play a five-letter "horse" game.
A third variation is to use the team name.

Taps Competition

Players pair off at a basket with one ball. One player has the ball at the free throw line. The partner stands in the first lane space on either side of the basket. The shooter continues shooting free throws until missing. One point is scored for each free throw made. On a miss, the rebounder is allowed two taps to score. If made, two points are awarded for the tap and players switch positions. If the rebounder fails to tap in the missed free throw, the free throw shooter continues shooting.

Variations: Games are played to 21 points. A second variation is to play a time limit game.

"321" Competition

Players pair off at a basket. Three points are scored for a jump shot at the free throw line. Two points are scored for a shot made outside the lane on either side of the basket. One point is scored for a layup. Partners alternate turns shooting until they score 21 points. They start at half court and dribble to the foul line for a jumper to begin. After that they may shoot from any spot to score 21 points.

Variations: The least number of shots needed to score 21 points is declared the winner.

A second variation is to time the players to see how much time it takes to score 21 points.

A third variation is to start and stop all players together. The winner at each basket is the player scoring the most points in the allotted time.

Inside-Outside Shooting

Players pair off and alternate turns shooting at a basket. There are ten shooting spots designated around the basket:

1. Right-hand layup off the backboard
2. Left-hand layup off the backboard
3. Left lane backboard shot
4. Straight shot from bottom of the free throw circle
5. Right lane backboard shot
6. Right baseline jump shot even with the basket
7. Right wing jump shot from fifteen feet
8. Top of the key jump shot
9. Left wing jump shot from fifteen feet
10. Left baseline jump shot even with the basket

Variations: Players start at spot one and continue in order. They shoot one shot at each spot. The most number of shots made from the ten spots is the winner.

A second variation is to shoot around the course and see how many consecutive shots they can make in a row.

A third variation is to count the number of shots needed to make one basket at each of the ten spots.

Spot Shot Score

Players split up evenly at all available baskets. Seven spots are marked off on the floor with different point values (Diagram 12-7).

A partner at each basket starts with a ball at half court. On your whistle, players drive to the top of the key for a jump shot. For a period of one minute, the shooter moves to any spot and tries to score as many points as possible.

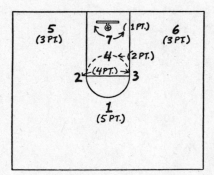

Diagram 12-7

Variations: Players must shoot at least one shot from each spot or the score does not count.

A second variation is to keep a basket total for both players combined to have partners competition.

RAPID SHOOTING RELEASE

The ability of getting the shot off quickly in balance and under control is a valuable asset. Many times a split second is the difference between scoring or getting the shot blocked. It is especially important to develop speed in the shooting release when receiving a pass and shooting off the dribble.

Quick Release Concentration

Players are assigned to groups of three at a basket. Two balls are used. Player A is the shooter and is stationed in the right corner along the baseline. Player B is the passer stationed on the free throw line. Player C is the rebounder stationed in the lane near the basket (Diagram 12-8).

A and B start with a basketball. A shoots a jump shot and immediately looks for a pass from B after landing. C rebounds all shots and passes to B. B continuously passes to A for jump shots. The drill runs for thirty seconds after which players rotate positions. The next time around the shooter switches to the left corner.

Variations: The shooter is on the wing with the passer at the top of the key and the rebounder in the lane.

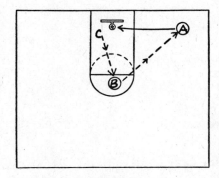

Diagram 12-8

A second variation is positioning the shooter at the top of the key with the passer in the wing area and the rebounder in the lane.

Juncture to Juncture

Players organize in groups of three at a basket. One player stands at the juncture of the free throw line and free throw lane on the right side. The other two players stand in the lane under the basket with a ball. The drill starts with the shooter taking a jump shot from the right juncture. Immediately after shooting the player moves quickly to the other juncture to receive the second ball for a jump shot. For a thirty-second period the player shoots and moves back and forth from juncture to juncture attempting to score as many baskets as possible. Players rotate positions after the time limit is up. The winner of the group is the player making the most shots.

Variation: Players must make a specific number of jump shots in the designated time.

Lane to Lane

Players pair off at a basket with one ball. One player starts with the ball outside the lane on the left side of the basket. On your signal, a shot is taken. Immediately the shooter recovers the ball and quickly moves outside the lane on the other side of the basket to shoot. The shooter attempts to make as many shots as possible moving back and forth across the lane for a thirty-second period of time. Partners alternate turns with losers assigned a sprint after the competition.

Free Throw Line Touch

Players pair off at a basket. One partner starts with a basketball underneath the basket and faces the free throw line. On your signal, the shooter dribbles out to touch the free throw line and immediately dribbles back to the basket for a layup. Rebounding the shot, the player dribbles back out to the foul line and back again for a layup. This continues for thirty seconds. Partners alternate turns with losers assigned a sprint.

Variations: Players shoot right-hand layups only.
Players shoot left-hand layups only.

A third variation is for the shooter to dribble out to the free throw line and take a jump shot.

A fourth variation is for the shooter to alternate moving out to the junctures on the left and right side each time they return to shoot.

13
Improving offensive transition techniques

Offensive transitions and fast-break situations develop instantaneously during a game. The continuity of an offensive exchange is predicated on the reaction-type movement initiated by a team's quick transition. Offensively players must be alert and ready to respond to court position and possession of the ball in establishing floor balance. The resulting action may be an easy score and applying additional pressure on the defense.

EVEN SITUATION TRANSITIONS

In many cases an offensive transition develops with an equal number of players on defense. Proper positioning of players and ball movement can create scoring opportunities even though the number of defensive players does not outnumber the defense. In addition, these situations are excellent conditioners.

Three-on-Three-on-Three

Divide the team into groups of three. Three teams at a time play a competitive game against each other. Team C has a basketball at half court. Team A is assigned to one basket and team B is assigned to the other basket (Diagram 13-1).

Team C advances the ball against team B and attempts to score. If C scores, B takes the ball out of bounds. C applies defensive pressure to the inbounds pass. Once the ball is inbounds, B moves upcourt to attack team A and tries to score. If C does not score, B rebounds and moves immediately upcourt against team A. C remains at the basket on defense to play against A when they have possession. The three-on-three game alternates back and forth until one team scores three baskets.

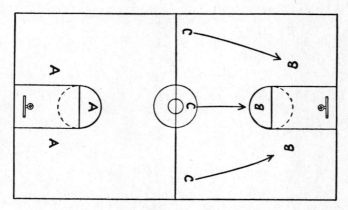

Diagram 13-1

Four-on-Four-on-Four

Divide the team into groups of four. Three groups at a time play a competitive game against each other. The same rules apply as in the three-on-three-on-three game.

Variation: Once the ball is in offensive scoring position, the team must execute a pass-and-screen-away maneuver or a pass-and-out maneuver before attempting to score.

Five-on-Five-on-Five

Divide the team into groups of five. Three groups at a time play a competitive game against each other. The same rules apply as in the previous two games.

Variation: The offensive team must execute their pattern offense to score if a quick score opportunity does not present itself.

UNEVEN SITUATION TRANSITIONS

Conditions develop in a game in which the offense outnumbers the defense in potential scoring situations. The offense must quickly adjust and attempt to take advantage of the situation. Games can be organized to produce continuous transition-type situations to give players experience in making the necessary adjustments to attack offensively.

Three-on-Two-on-Two

Station an offensive team of three players at half court with a ball. Assign two players on defense to both baskets (Diagram 13-2).

Offensive team A advances the ball in either direction and attempts to score against the defense. If they score, the ball is taken out-of-bounds and immediately moved upcourt against the other pair of defenders. The offense moves back and forth full court against both defenses and attempts to score three to five baskets in a designated time period.

Any time the defense rebounds a missed shot or intercepts the ball, the ball is immediately dropped to the floor. The offense recovers it quickly and advances the ball in the opposite direction. If the defense knocks the ball out-of-bounds, one of the offensive players quickly passes the ball inbounds and the ball is moved in the opposite direction. The defense always applies pressure to the ball on their side of half court.

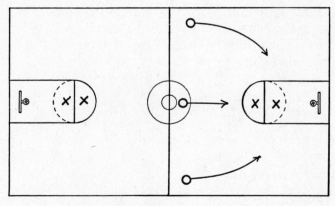

Diagram 13-2

Four-on-Three-on-Three

The offensive team of four players attempts to score against three defenders at either end. The same rules in the three-on-two-on-two game apply.

Five-on-Four-on-Four

The offensive team of five players attempts to score against four defenders at either end. The same game rules previously mentioned apply.

FAST-BREAK SITUATIONS

Developing fast-break situations to score quickly and keep the defense off balance is an important part of offensive basketball. Quick scores in transition can demoralize the opponent and help alleviate defensive pressure.

Filling the Alleys

The players are stationed on the end line in three lines. You are at the free throw line with a basketball (Diagrams 13-3, 13-4).

In option A, you pass the ball to the middle player. The receiver passes immediately to either wing. The wing dribbles up the middle of the floor. The passer cuts behind and moves up the sideline to become the new wing. The dribbler stops at the free throw line and passes to the opposite wing cutting in toward the basket for a layup.

In option B, you pass to either wing. The receiver immediately dribbles to the middle and up the center of the court. The middle player cuts behind the dribbler to the outside and replaces in the wing position. The dribbler stops at the free throw line and passes to the opposite wing cutting in toward the basket for a layup.

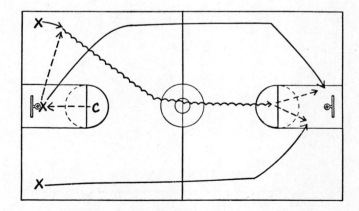

Diagram 13-3

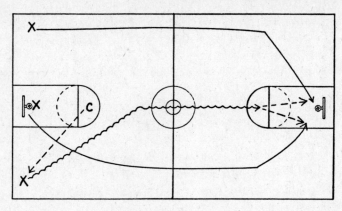

Diagram 13-4

Pitchout and Follow

Divide the squad into two groups on the end of the court. Group A is lined up out-of-bounds underneath the basket. Group B is lined up out-of-bounds where the end line and sideline meet (Diagram 13-5).

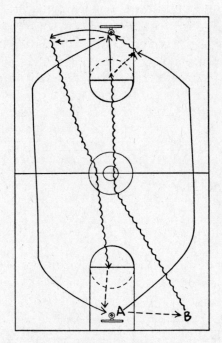

Diagram 13-5

A steps inbounds with a basketball and tosses the ball off the backboard. A then times a jump to recover it. A immediately outlet passes to B in the corner. B proceeds to dribble to the middle of the court and up the floor. A cuts behind B and streaks down the sideline. When B reaches the free throw line a pass is thrown to A for a layup. After shooting, A continues out to the corner. B follows in for the rebound and outlet passes to A in the corner. The action is now reversed with A dribbling up the middle of the floor. B moves down the sideline to receive a pass for a layup. The drill action is continuous with the second group in line starting when the first group crosses over half court. After three minutes, the corner group switches to the other side of the court. The ball is advanced from the left side and a left-handed layup is shot.

Three-on-Two with a Stationary Defense

Divide the squad in half. Station both groups at opposite ends of the court (Diagram 13-6).

Players 1, 2, and 3 fill the lanes and run a fast break against A and B until they score. On a made shot or rebounded miss, A or B passes to C breaking to midcourt, and all three fast-break against 4 and 5 who have already moved into defensive position at the other end. Players 1, 2, and 3 step off the court and go to the end of the line behind D, E, and F. Players D and E step on the court for defense when the break comes back. The drill is run continuously back and forth for five minutes.

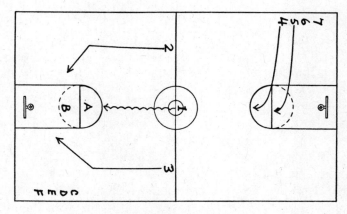

Diagram 13-6

Three-on-Two with a Back-Pedaling Defense

Divide the squad in half with both groups stationed at half court. The rotation and flow of the players occur from either the left or right side depending on the outlet pass (Diagram 13-7).

Players 1, 2, and 3 start the drill by fast-breaking against A and B. The two players not directly involved in the last possession of the ball recover downcourt to play defense. Player 1 shoots and scores. Players 2 and 3 immediately back pedal downcourt to play defense. A or B passes the ball to midcourt to C or 4, depending on which side of the basket the ball is recovered. Players A, B, and C or 4 fast-break against 2 and 3. The fast-break action is continuous with the players stepping off the court and going to the end of the line from which the new player came. The drill is run for five minutes.

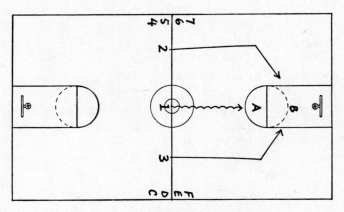

Diagram 13-7

Team Exchange

The players line up in eleven positions on the floor. Any extra team members line up on the sideline behind the wing position (Diagram 13-8).

Players 1, 2, and 3 at midcourt advance the ball toward 4 and 5 in a three-on-two fast break. On any change of possession (made shot, missed shot, turnover, steal), the player with the ball passes to the sideline player (8 or 10) on the side of the basket the ball is rebounded or recovered. The rebounder along with 8 and 10 break down against 6 and 7. The players who just finished fast breaking fill in the open positions on the floor as quickly as possible to be ready for the next exchange. The drill is run for five minutes as all players react and fill the open positions on the floor after completion of their play.

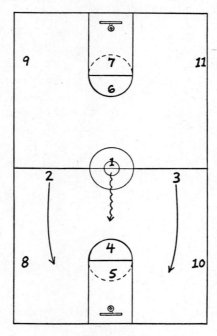

Diagram 13-8

Four-on-Three Fast Break and Exchange

Three players (1-2-3) set up in a defensive shell. Four players (A-B-C-D) are assigned on offense with a ball. The rest of the squad is divided in half, out-of-bounds at midcourt on both sidelines (Diagram 13-9).

A, B, C, and D fast-break against 1, 2, and 3. When the defense gets a rebound or a shot is made, the ball is immediately passed to the first player in line at midcourt. The pass is made to the closest sideline determined by the position of the ball when recovered. The three defenders plus the sideline player fast-break the other way. The player who shot from the first group drops out while the three remaining offensive players recover to play defense. A continuous four-on-three break is run back and forth for five minutes.

Variation: The same drill can be organized to produce a continuous five-on-four fast break. Player positioning is the same except that four players start on defense and five start on offense. The same adjustment is made with the pass to midcourt after a change of possession.

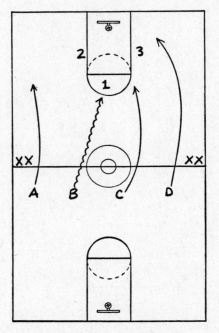

Diagram 13-9

Fast Break Fill-In

The entire squad is involved in a continuous fast-break adjustment drill. Players A, B, and C form a cup around the basket to initiate a three-player fast-break off a rebound. Players D and E are stationed at midcourt to defense the fast break as it develops. The rest of the squad is positioned out-of-bounds at midcourt (Diagram 13-10).

A three-on-two fast break is started. Three situations can happen that will dictate the offensive and defensive adjustments to continue the drill and involve the sideline players. They are:

1. A shot will be made by the offensive team.
2. A shot will be missed and rebounded by the defense.

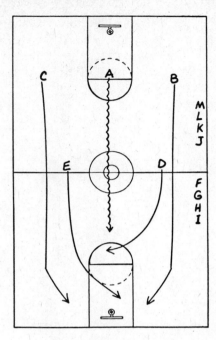

Diagram 13-10

3. The ball will be turned over to the defensive team without a shot being taken, because of a bad pass, poor pass reception, defensive steal, violation, or offensive foul. To save time, if a foul is committed by the defensive team, it is treated as a shot made.

The rules of action for the drill are:

1. If a shot is made, the shooter moves off the court to the end of the line. The remaining players become the defense in the next fast-break situation. Example: Players A, B, and C break againt players D and E. Player A makes a shot and moves off the court to the end of the line. Players B and C remain on the floor to defense the next fast break against D, E, and F, who has moved on the court to join them.

2. If a shot is missed and a defensive rebound is secured, only the player missing the shot remains on the floor to defense the next fast break. The rest of the players on offense move off the court and go to the end of the line. Example: Players A, B, and C fast break against players D and E. A misses a shot and D rebounds. A remains on the floor to defense D and E in a two-on-one break (Diagram 13-11).

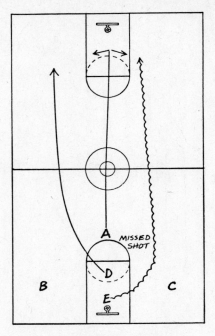

Diagram 13-11

3. If the ball is turned over to the defense without a shooting attempt, all offensive players remain on the floor to defense the next break. Example: Players A, B, and C throw the ball away during the three-on-two break against D and E. A, B, and C remain on the floor and recover quickly to defense the next fast break. To create an offensive advantage, players F and G join D and E to create a four-on-three break (Diagram 13-12).

The drill continues with the players filling in from midcourt to form the various fast-break situations that will occur depending upon what happens on the floor. The sequence of possible fast-break situations are:

1. An original three-on-two situation remains three-on-two if a shot is made. A missed shot creates a two-on-one. A turnover becomes a four-on-three break.

2. An original two-on-one situation remains two-on-one if a shot is made. A missed shot results in a two-on-one. A turnover becomes a three-on-two break.

3. An original four-on-three break continues if a shot is made. A missed shot results in a three-on-one. A turnover becomes a five-on-four break.

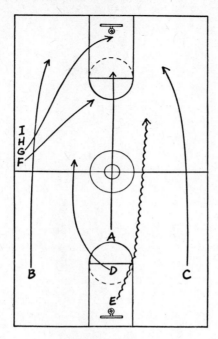

Diagram 13-12

Note: If a turnover results in a five-on-four break, a five-on-four remains by removing the shooter, or the drill ends and starts over with a three-on-two. The players move to the court on either offense or defense depending on what happens on the break.

OFFENSIVE TEAM TRANSITIONS

The most important point about offensive transitions is that every player must get involved and move quickly upcourt as soon as their team gets possession of the ball. In order to score, a team must be aggressive and attack on offense to take advantage of scoring opportunities when they develop. Often, a fast score will occur on the quick offensive transition before the defense has a chance to recover and set up.

Four-on-Four Scramble Score

Divide the squad into groups of four. O is offense and X is defense. Both groups mix inside the free throw lane and do not stand next to their assigned opponent (Diagram 13-13).

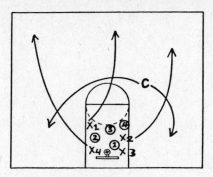

Diagram 13-13

You have a ball and shoot from different spots on the floor. Whoever rebounds the shot is on offense with the rest of the team. They spread out quickly and fast-break to the far basket. The defense quickly locates their assignment and attempts to recover and prevent a score. When the offense scores or the defense gets possession, play stops. Both groups spread out in the lane again waiting for you to take another shot.

Variations: Toss the ball off the backboard and call the name of the team to be on offense.

A second variation is for you to toss the ball into the lane and call the name of the player to get possession.

Five-on-Five Scramble Score

Break the squad into groups of five. The players spread out and move around inside the lane as in the previous drill. Each player has a guarding assignment for defensive purposes. You shoot the ball to start the first series. The team rebounding the ball is immediately on offense and breaks downcourt to score. The other team recovers quickly to pick up their assignent and play defense. The continuous breaking back and forth continues until one team or the other scores. On any turnover or change of possession, the direction of play is also changed until one team or the other scores. After any score, the players move back into the free throw lane again and wait for another series to start with a shot by you.

Variations: Toss the ball into the lane and call which team is to be on offense first.

A second variation is for you to toss the ball to a specific player to designate which team is on offense.

Fire and Fly

Divide the squad into groups of four. Each group attempts to score as many baskets as possible in two minutes. There is no defensive opposition. Play starts when one of the players from a group shoots a jump shot from the free throw line. The following restrictions are employed during the two-minute duration:

1. After the first shot to start, all players must be over half court when each succeeding shot is taken.
2. The first shot taken at each basket is from the free throw line. If missed, the second shot must be taken outside the free throw lane on the side. If missed, the third shot may be taken from anywhere.
3. The ball is taken out-of-bounds on the end line by any player after a score. The first pass inbounds must be made inside the free throw line. The second pass must be made to a player between the free throw line and half court. The third pass can be made anywhere over half court. However, before the first shot is taken at the free throw line, all players must be over half court.

Variations: The drill is run with three players for a one-minute period.

A second variation is to run the drill with five players for a three-minute period.

Team Pass and Go

Divide the squad into five player units. One unit has the ball on offense. The other unit is on defense (Diagram 13-14).

The offensive unit (O) spreads around the perimeter in a three-two formation. The defensive unit is in position on their individual guarding assignment. The offense begins passing the ball around the perimeter. They are allowed to skip pass the person next to them. The defensive unit (X) reacts to the ball in adjusting their stance and position in relation to the basket. However, the defense is not allowed to intercept the ball. After several passes, yell "shot" or "recover." On the "shot" command, the offense immediatley takes a shot. If the shot is made, the defense immediately takes the ball out-of-bounds and breaks upcourt. The offense recovers to play defense. If the shot is

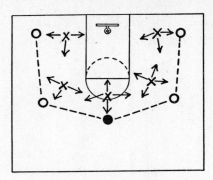

Diagram 13-14

missed, the defense rebounds and breaks upcourt. In either case, the passing formation is set up again until another command is given. If you call "recover," the next player receiving a pass will toss the ball to the defender of that player. The teams switch offense and defense immediately on the transition up the floor. Once again the passing formation is set up until you call another command.

Transition Scoring

The squad divides into five player units. Each time a unit comes on the floor the players alternate starting on offense and defense to begin the drill. Three players have a basketball on offense (O). The remaining two players (X) set up in a one-one tandem on defense (Diagram 13-15).

The offense begins by running a three-on-two break against the defense. The two defenders, after getting possession of the ball, break back on offense. One of the three original offensive players recovers on defense against the two. This player is determined by:

1. The player taking the last shot before the defense gains possession.

2. The player making a shot.

3. A player throwing a bad pass.

4. A player creating a violation.

After the two-on-one break is completed, the lone defender grabs the rebound or made shot and immediately sprint dribbles full court for a layup.

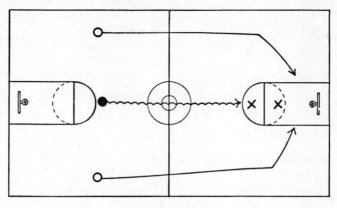

Diagram 13-15

GAME SITUATION TRANSITIONS

Many specific situations occur in every game including jump balls, free throws, live-ball and dead-ball turnovers. Transitions off these situations in the form of breakdown drills will familiarize players with the appropriate reaction to take advantage of immediate possession.

Jump Ball Recovery

The squad divides into five player units. Player matchups are designated by you. Various formations on jump ball situations are practiced. On all matchups you designate the opposing jumpers. Each team lines up and reacts to the direction of the tap to gain possession. All players are matched up to have an opportunity in a jump ball. Develop all possibilities including an offensive tap certainty, a defensive tap probability, and a neutral tap situation.

Variations: Players on the circle match up with their opponent on their right shoulder. They rotate to the left on the toss and break to the far basket as soon as they gain possession.

A second variation is for the players to match up with their opponent on their left shoulder. They rotate to the right on the toss and break to the far basket as soon as they gain possession.

A third variation is to set up offensive and defensive

situations at a basket with the team moving full court for a shot after gaining possession.

A fourth variation is to set up neutral jump ball situations at midcourt.

A fifth variation is to set up jump ball situations in as many lineups as possible including box, diamond, triangle, and wide formations to expose players to the many situations they may encounter in a game.

Turnover Reaction

Divide the squad into five player scrimmage units. One unit is on offense and one on defense. The offensive unit starts with the basketball and remains on offense as long as they score or do not lose possession by a turnover. When the defense rebounds a missed shot, play stops immediately and the defensive team goes on offense in the next series. Play continues in the same fashion with both units executing the offensive patterns designated by you. The offense and defense continue switching as missed shots are rebounded. When a live turnover (bad pass, defensive interception, steal, blocked shot, etc.) occurs, the defensive unit immediately attacks by moving the ball full court to the opposite basket. The offensive unit must make a quick transition on the turnover in pursuit and play defense to stop an easy basket. The half-court offense is set up and run again until another turnover occurs and the action is extended into a full-court transition.

Variation: The scrimmage operates at half court until you sound a whistle. The offensive player with the ball drops it and the entire unit recovers on defense.

Free Throw Adjustment

Divide the squad into five player scrimmage units. One unit is designated offense (O) and lines up in an offensive free throw shooting alignment. The other unit (X) lines up in a defensive arrangement (Diagram 13-16).

Each player in turn on offense shoots a one-and-one free throw. The rest of the players rotate and set up in the appropriate lane positions according to their size and your philosophy. If a free throw is missed and the offensive team rebounds, they set up their half-court offense and run one series. If the defense rebounds a missed free throw, they move quickly to the far basket and run one offensive series off the half-court offense. After the series, they set up in the offensive free throw shooting positions and shoot one-and-ones while rotating. The next miss determines which team is on offense.

Variation: The team rebounding a missed free throw sets up on offense at the same basket by moving the ball out of traffic and into the offensive formation.

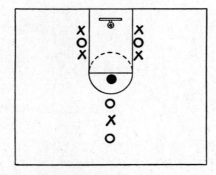

Diagram 13-16

14

Improving offensive team play through scrimmage methods and techniques

Successful basketball teams employ the total team play concept. In order to achieve consistency in team performance, the skills and abilities of all players must be taken into account and incorporated into developing the offensive and defensive patterns. There is little room for specialization in basketball. Players must be able to play all phases and contribute to the overall scheme of the game.

Total player involvement develops responsibility, discipline, and control. Players must learn to recognize their limitations as well as accent their strengths in contributing to the success of the team. Balanced scoring potential is a key to scoring consistency and involving all players in the part of the game that is the most fun. Defense, rebounding, and scoring are the most important areas where the total team effort is essential.

Practice situations properly organized will develop and emphasize the importance of all players in the team's performance. Particularly important in teaching team play is to structure the various half- and full-court scrimmage conditions under guidelines to develop concentration and emphasize the importance of ball possession and proper shot selection on offense. You can isolate specific restrictions to motivate players to perform at peak effort. This will help develop proper playing habits, which are necessary for team and individual success.

DUMMY WORK CONCENTRATION

The term "dummy" implies here the isolation of specific patterns without any opposition. The purpose is to emphasize the development of confidence, understanding, and timing. It is particularly important to use the "dummy" concept when learning new patterns and making improvements or adjustments on already established patterns.

Offensive Pattern Execution

The squad splits into five player units. Each unit is assigned to a basket. All units simultaneously execute the team offensive patterns while concentration on timing, rhythm, and continuity. The first unit executes the desired pattern at a main basket under your careful scrutiny for initial learning and correction. After a specific time or number of repetitions, they move to the opposite basket and continue executing the pattern. The second unit steps on the court to run the pattern at the first basket. After a period of time, the second unit moves to the opposite basket. The third unit begins with you while the first unit steps off the court to observe. Each specific pattern is practiced in the same fashion as units rotate. Shooting the basketball is not allowed, as the emphasis of the drill is on the continuity and execution of the pattern. The following conditions are imposed for learning and developing proper execution:

1. After the pattern is in progress and proper movement established, a whistle by you signals a shot is to be taken as players scramble to their rebounding and potential defensive positioning.
2. A designated number of passes must be made before a shot is taken. This allows sufficient time to check player positioning and responsibility.
3. Every player must touch the ball before a shot is taken.

Out-of-Bounds Pattern Execution

Divide the squad into two units of players. Both main baskets are used simultaneously. Indicate which specific out-of-bounds series is to be run. All players execute the pattern by rotating positions on the floor as well as being the inbounds passer. After a period of time, the reserves in each unit rotate in to run the pattern. Call out each out-of-bounds pattern to run in sequence. Each specific option is executed to conclusion before a shot is taken. The following out-of-bounds situations are emphasized in detail:

1. The offensive basket series against all types of defenses with the ball being inbounded from both the left and right side of the basket.

2. The sideline out-of-bounds series is executed from both the fore-court and backcourt areas to emphasize positional changes be-cause of the different position of the ball. The inbounds pass is made from both the left and right side of the court with all players making the pass in.

3. The end line out-of-bounds series against all types of defenses and pressure are executed. Time and score factors are taken into consideration with the ball being passed inbounds from both the left and right side of the basket.

Zone Offense Concentration

Split the squad into two units. Units execute simultaneously at the main baskets. You designate which offensive pattern to execute. The ball is moved quickly without shooting or dribbling. On a whistle, the next player receiving the ball takes a shot. Players move into rebounding position and retrieve the ball before it hits the floor. Substitutions are made after the play is completed; ball movement is continued on your command until the next whistle dictates a shot and player substitutions.

Variations: A specific number of passes must be completed before a shot is taken.

A second variation is that every player must touch the ball before a shot is taken.

A third variation is to start the ball on the left side and reverse it to the right side before a shot is taken. On the next series, the situation is reversed.

HALF-COURT SCRIMMAGE METHODS AND TECHNIQUES

The development of team offensive patterns must be concen-trated in half-court scrimmage methods and techniques. This allows the offensive teams many more opportunities to develop continuity of action as well as reinforcing team play concepts and basic knowledge. Specific offensive options may be isolated and the players receive more concentration on making appropriate adjustments dictated by defensive changes.

Consecutive Offensive Opportunities

Split the squad into two units. A half-court scrimmage situation is set up. The scrimmage remains exclusively at one basket. The offensive unit receives five opportunities before switching with the defense. A ratio of scoring conversions is kept to provide motivation for maximum effort and execution. After the units flip-flop, substitutions on each unit are made. After each specific offensive series, the ball is returned to the top of the key before the next series is started.

Time Allotment Scrimmage

The squad is split into two units. A half-court scrimmage situation is set up. The offensive unit is given the basketball for a specific time period. Each time they score, the ball is brought back to the top of the key to begin play again. Whenever the defensive rebounds or stops the play, the offense is given the ball back at the top of the key. After the time limit has elapsed, the units switch offense and defense. Score of conversions is kept for both units. Substitutions are made after both units have been on offense and defense.

Variations: The offensive team is given two minutes to score. Every time they score or the defense gets possession, the clock is stopped. The clock starts again when the ball is put back into play at the top of the key. Keep score.

A second variation is to keep the percentage of conversions when the units are on offense.

Offense-Repetition-Score

Divide the squad into two units for half-court scrimmaging. Each unit selects their best free throw shooter to start the scrimmage. Free throws are matched to determine which team gets possession of the ball to start. The offensive unit will stay on offense as long as they score. The defense attempts to prevent the offense from scoring without fouling. When they get possession of the ball by stopping the offense, they move on offense. If the offensive unit scores three times in a row, the defensive unit is assigned some form of sprints while the offense rests.

Missed Shot-Substitution

Split the squad into two units for half-court play. A match of free throws determines which unit starts on offense first. The offensive unit remains on offense as long as they score. The defense must stop a score without fouling to get on offense. Substitutions are automatically made on missed shots as play is stopped while the ball is returned to the top of the key. Players off the court are numbered consecutively 1-2-3-4, etc. Number 1 replaces the first player who misses on either team. Number 2 replaces the next player who misses. The players missing a shot move off the court and fall in behind the players who are waiting to get into the scrimmage. This is an excellent method to interchange players on different units to improve team play and familiarity with all team members.

Missed Shot—Free Throw—Substitution

Split the squad into two units for half-court play. The unit starting on offense is determined by a match of free throws. The offensive unit stays on offense while they score. Each time a shot is missed, a substitution is made for the shooter as units change from offense to defense. On a made shot, the shooter steps to the free throw line. Both units line up in a free throw shooting situation. If the free throw is made, the team remains on offense. If missed, a substitution is made for the shooter. As previously mentioned, players are assigned numbers to establish their order into the scrimmage.

Designated Restrictions

Divide the squad into two units for half-court scrimmaging. A match of free throws determines which unit starts on defense. They remain on offense while they score by performing the designated restrictions outlined by you.

1. Chest passes only are allowed.
2. Bounce passes only are allowed.

3. Only three dribbles are allowed per player per possession unless penetration is made for a layup.
4. No shots are allowed outside the free throw line. Substitutions are made on missed shots and/or violating the restrictions as the units switch offense and defense.

FULL-COURT SCRIMMAGE METHODS AND TECHNIQUES

Full-court scrimmaging under control conditions is vital in developing the transitional phase of basketball. Moving the ball up quickly on offense and recovering quickly on defense are team-oriented goals that will be developed through concentrated full-court scrimmaging in practice sessions.

Regulation Game Control Conditions

Divide the squad into two units for scrimmaging. The first five for each unit line up in a jump ball at center court. Conduct a three-minute regulation full-court scrimmage. Stop the clock on all dead-ball situations. When the time limit is up, substitutions are made and the ball is put into play with a jump ball again at center court. A series of two, three-minute scrimmage sessions with a thirty- to forty-five second rest period between as the reserves on both units are moved into the scrimmage. Each time the scrimmage period is over, the teams switch baskets for the next period.

Captain(s) Draft

As a change of pace, have the captain(s) draft teams before practice starts. Make sure that forwards and guards are evenly split on both squads. Conduct a regulation full-court scrimmage under normal game conditions. Keep score. The period of time between substitutions varies from two to three minutes. The captains act as coaches and determine which players are in and out each time substitutions are made. Teams switch baskets after each period. Captains agree on a suitable penalty for the losing team. During the scrimmage the score is kept, statistics are charted, and conversion percentage is totaled to emphasize the importance of good shot selection.

Coach's Choice

Two units are organized with the coach aligning different combinations on players and appropriate defensive assignments. Four-minute scrimmage sessions are conducted under game conditions. After each scrimmage period, different scrimmage units are developed.

1. The first team vs. the second team.
2. The first team guards and second team forwards vs. the first team forwards and second team guards.
3. Left-handers vs. right-handers.
4. Juniors vs. seniors.
5. Guards vs. guards and forwards vs. forwards.

Squad Rotation

Fourteen players are utilized in a full-court scrimmage. Two five-player units scrimmage at one basket. The remaining four players are stationed at the other basket (Diagram 14-1).

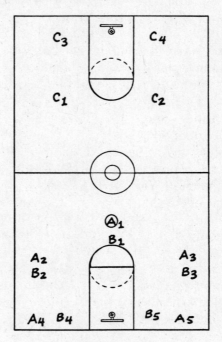

Diagram 14-1

Use game conditions in the scrimmage. The offense stays on offense at the same basket as long as they score. On a missed shot or a turnover, the defensive team advances the ball full court against the four-player unit that is already in position. The fifth player to join their unit is the player who missed the shot or turned the ball over at the other end. This player must recover quickly to get back on defense. The remaining four players wait at the other end to play defense on the next exchange. The scrimmage session is run eight to ten minutes. Individual shooting and turnover statistics are kept.

HALF-FULL COURT SCRIMMAGE ADJUSTMENTS

A combination of the advantages realized in half-court work and full-court work are applied in the half-court adjustment series. Emphasize concentration on pattern execution and good shot selection in the half-court scrimmaging phase. Expand this to include offensive and defensive transitions in the full-court phase, which becomes an automatic adjustment when the half-court phase breaks down.

Half-Court Made—Full-Court Miss

Split the squad into three units. Depending on the number of squad members, some players will have to double on different units. Two units begin scrimmaging for a four-minute session. After matching free throws to determine the first possession, the offensive unit stays on offense at the same basket while they score. On a missed shot or turnover, a full-court transition is made with the defensive unit advancing the ball to go on offense and the offensive unit recovering on defense. After the time limit is up, the unit scoring the most baskets steps off the court. The third unit steps on the floor and starts the next period on offense.

Designate the Rebound

Divide the squad into three units. Two units step on the floor inside the free throw lane around the basket in rebounding position. You have a basketball outside the free throw lane and attempt a shot from anywhere on the perimeter. Both units scramble for the rebound. The team which successfully retrieves the ball then clears the ball out and sets up their offense at the same basket. They execute their patterns and stay on offense while they score. When they fail to score or turn the ball over, play stops and both units step back inside the free throw lane to rebound. After five rebounds, the unit off the floor steps on to replace a unit. Each unit is rotated in order until they all rebound against one another. The second time around the emphasis is on defensive rebounding. This time the team rebounding the ball moves full court quickly to set up their offense. The nonrebounding unit recovers full court to play defense. When the offense fails to score, play is over and the teams move back inside the free throw lane to rebound.

PATTERN ISOLATION

Isolating specific patterns is a great aid in learning and developing the offensive and defensive system. By isolating patterns through controlled scrimmaging conditions, much concentrated emphasis can be placed on specific areas. This constant reinforcement is a tremendous aid in developing the team concept of play.

Press Offense Concentration

Divide the squad into two units. The first seven players are on unit one and the rest of the squad is on unit two. You designate which five players will start for each unit. Both units start by stepping inside the free throw lane. Players move around in the lane to mix up their assignments. Call out a player's name or team. The unit designated quickly sets up their offense against a press. The other unit sets up to press defensively. When both teams are organized, hand the ball to a player out-of-bounds to start the play. Conduct a visible five-second count. Play continues until the ball is prevented from being put inbounds within the allotted time, the offense fails to get the ball over half court within ten seconds, a turnover, or the offense successfully moves the ball into their half-court offense. At the conclusion of play, all players move back into the free throw lane for the next call. After three series of situations, substitutions are made.

One-Half Court Press Offense

Divide the squad into three units. All units rotate from defense to offense and off the court after three opportunities to press defensively and attack offensively. Place a basketball at either end of the court out-of-bounds behind the end line. Players from two units randomly spread out around the midcourt area (Diagram 14-2).

Yell which team is on offense and point to the end from which the ball will be taken out. Immediately an offensive player sprints to the end line to pass the ball inbounds. The defensive team meanwhile sets up in a one-half court press and waits for the offense to advance the ball up against them. Play is over when one of three conditions exist:

1. The ten-second count is violated in backcourt by the offense.
2. The defense intercepts the ball or forces a turnover.
3. The offense completes three passes in the forecourt while setting up in their half-court offense.

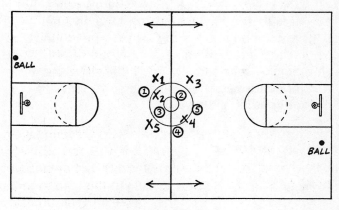

Diagram 14-2

Three-Quarter Court Press Offense

Divide the squad into three units. The units rotate from defense to offense and off the court after three opportunities each. Some players will have to double in different units because of squad size. Players from two units are stationed inside the free throw lane in a mixed arrangement. After the designation of offense and defense determined by you, the defensive unit hustles to set up a three-quarter court press originating at the free throw line. The offensive team moves to their positions on the floor. Present the ball and start a five-second visible count. Play stops when one of four conditions exist:

1. The five-second count elapses before the ball is touched inbounds.
2. The ten-second count is violated in backcourt.
3. The defensive team intercepts the ball or causes a turnover.
4. The offensive team penetrates the press and sets up their half-court offense.

Variations: Both units set up the press off a free throw shooting situation.

A second variation is for the units to set up the press after a made field goal.

Full-Court Zone Press Offense

Split the squad into three units. All units rotate from defense to offense and off the court, after three opportunities to press and attack. Stand with a basketball out-of-bounds on the end line. The players from two units are standing in the free throw lane around the basket. Call out the team or individual to take the ball out-of-bounds. The defensive unit quickly reacts to set up a full-court zone press. Hand the ball to the inbounds passer after the defense is set. Play continues until one of four conditions prevail:

1. The five-second inbounds time limit is violated.
2. The ten-second backcourt count is violated.
3. The defense intercepts the ball or forces a turnover.
4. The offense successfully advances the ball into forecourt.

Sideline Out-of-Bounds Series

Split the squad into three units. All units rotate from defense to offense and off the court. After three opportunities each to run the sideline out-of-bounds play, groups switch. A ball is placed on the floor out-of-bounds on both sidelines. Players from two units randomly spread out around the midcourt area. You call the team or individual to take the ball out-of-bounds. Indicate the sideline and basket toward which the offense will move. The defensive unit picks up their individual assignments as quickly as possible. Start a five-second count as soon as the ball is picked up, and play continues until:

1. The five-second inbounds time limit is violated.
2. The ball is passed into backcourt and prevented from being thrown into forecourt within ten seconds.

3. The defense intercepts the ball or causes a turnover.
4. The offense scores directly off the play or advances the ball into forecourt and sets up in the normal half-court offense.

Jump Ball Conditions

Split the squad into three units. All units rotate against each other after several opportunities. Two units are lined up in a jump ball situation at the center circle. You designate the two jumpers. Both units line up according to the conditions that exist. A certain possession indicates an offensive alignment. No chance for the tap indicates a pure defensive alignment. A "toss up" for possession indicates a neutral lineup to intercept the tap. The play is over when either team gains possesion and moves into position to set up the half-court offense. In addition to the center circle, jump ball situations are held at both the offensive and defensive baskets.

OVERLOAD SCRIMMAGE CONDITIONS

In order to improve execution and strengthen an offensive pattern, overloading is a valuable teaching aid. This places additional pressure on a specific unit and creates a better team awareness of player positioning and purpose.

Five-on-Six Defense

Split the squad into three offensive units. Each unit receives five opportunities to score against six defenders. The ball is put into play at the top of the key. The offensive unit employs normal offensive patterns to score against the six defenders. Score is kept by recording the number of successful attempts converted out of five opportunities each time a unit is on offense.

Five-on-Seven Defense

Divide the squad into three offensive units. Each unit receives three chances to penetrate and beat the defense for a score. Assign seven players defensive responsibilities at three-quarter court. Five of the players have individual assignments. The remaining two players free-lance by applying pressure in the middle of the floor against the offense. Play stops when:

1. The defense intercepts the ball or forces a turnover.
2. The defense forces a ten-second call in the backcourt.
3. The offense successfully advances the ball over half court and runs an offensive series to score.

Five-on-Eight Defense

Split the squad into five player units for offensive purposes. Eight players are assigned on defense. Each offensive unit has three opportunities before switching. The offensive unit sets up in their normal offensive pattern against a full-court zone press. The defense is aligned in a zone press arrangement. The additional three defenders are assigned to the following areas to apply extra pressure on the offense. One player is stationed between the end line and free throw line. A second player is stationed between the free throw line and half court. The third player is stationed between half court and the far free throw line. These defenders may only defense the ball within the boundary lines of their specific area. Play continues until:

1. The five-second inbounds count is violated.
2. The ten-second backcourt count is violated.
3. The defense intercepts the ball or forces a turnover.
4. The offense successfully gets the ball over half court and sets up in their offensive pattern.

LAST-SECOND GAME SITUATIONS

Many games throughout the season are decided in the final few seconds. Therefore, it is imperative that practice be designed to include the last-second situation strategy. Repetition of appropriate decision making will instill confidence in the players should that situation occur in a game. Although there are no guarantees in basketball, practice on special situations will at least acquaint the players with the possibilities that probably will occur in some games during the season.

Fast Break Off Free Throw

Split the squad into three units. The units are rotated after five opportunities on offense and defense. One unit lines up in an offensive free throw alignment. The second unit lines up defensively.

Each player on offense goes to the line for a free throw. If the shot is made, a player on the defensive team jumps out-of-bounds quickly and passes it in play. They attempt to get the ball downcourt and get a reasonable shot off in five seconds. If the free throw is missed, the defensive team rebounds and tries to get the ball downcourt for a shot within five seconds. After each player has shot a free throw, units rotate from offense to defense and off the court.

Three-Second Offense Basket Out-of-Bounds

Split the squad into two units. Units are switched from offense to defense after five opportunities. Substitutions are made after the switch. One unit is designated offense and sets up in their offensive basket out-of-bounds series. The other unit sets up in a defensive formation. Present the ball to the inbounds passer and start a five-second count. The ball is put into play with the clock starting as soon as the ball is touched inbounds. The offensive team must get a shot off in three seconds. Each player on offense passes the ball in from out-of-bounds once before units switch.

Four-Second Sideline Out-of-Bounds in Forecourt

Divide the squad into two units. The units are switched after five opportunities each on offense and defense. One unit is designated offense and sets up in their sideline out-of-bounds series. Each player on offense has one chance to pass the ball inbounds to start the series. Present the ball to the passer and start a visible five-second count. As soon as the ball is touched inbounds, the clock starts. Four seconds are allowed to get a reasonable shot off. Play is stopped when:

1. The five-second inbounds time limit is violated.
2. The ball is intercepted by the defense.
3. The four-second time limit elapses.

Five-Second Sideline Out-of-Bounds in Backcourt

Divide the squad into two units. The units are switched on offense and defense after five opportunities. The offensive unit takes the ball out-of-bounds on the sideline in backcourt. Present the ball to the inbounds passer and start a five-second count. When the ball is touched inbounds, start the clock and allow the offense five seconds to advance the ball into position for a good shot. Each unit gets five attempts to score with everyone taking the ball out-of-bounds before the units switch offense and defense. Play continues until:

1. The five-second inbounds time limit is violated.
2. The ball is intercepted by the defense.
3. The five-second time limit elapses for the shot when the ball is touched inbounds.

Six-Second End Line Out-of-Bounds

Divide the squad into two units. Offense and defense switch after five opportunities. The offense takes the ball out-of-bounds on the end line to start. They have six seconds to move the ball full court to get a good shot off. Each player passes the ball inbounds before the units switch offense and defense. You present the ball each time to the inbounds passer and start a five-second count. When the ball is touched inbounds, the clock is started and play continues until:

1. The ball is intercepted by the defense.
2. The six-second time limit elapses.

Last-Second Full-Court Out-of-Bounds

Divide the squad into three units. The units are rotated from offense to defense and off the court. Some players will be required to double in units depending upon the size of the squad. One unit lines up on offense taking the ball out-of-bounds on the end line. They have five seconds to get the ball downcourt for a good shot. The defensive unit will employ varioius type defenses according to time and score (one point behind, one point ahead, and tied). Present the ball out-of-bounds and start a five-second count. When the ball is touched inbounds, the clock will be started and a whistle sounded when the five-second time limit elapses. Units rotate after three opportunities to score.

Last-Second Out-of-Bounds at Half Court

Divide the squad into three units. Each unit receives three attempts on offense. Units rotate from offense to defense and off the court. The ball is presented out-of-bounds to the offense on the sideline at midcourt. The situation is four seconds remaining and a two-point deficit. The defensive unit is lined up in a zone. The clock starts once the ball is touched inbounds.

Last-Second Jump Ball Situations

Divide the squad into two units. Each unit has three matchups before substitutions are made. Both units line up for a jump ball at center court. You designate the jumpers so each unit will have an offensive advantage, defensive disadvantage, and a neutral tap situation. In each jump there are ten seconds remaining. Substitutions are made on both units after the units have switched offense and defense. The second set of jump ball situations occur at a basket with the following conditions and time limits in force:

1. An offensive advantage at the same basket with four seconds remaining and a one-point deficit.
2. An offensive advantage toward the far basket with seven seconds remaining and a one-point deficit.
3. A neutral tap situation with the score tied and five seconds remaining.

Index